Rabindranath Tagore
and
Crisis in Civilization

Rabindranath Tagore and Crisis in Civilization

Dr. R.K. Pruthi

FORWARD BOOKS
NEW DELHI-110002 (INDIA)

FORWARD BOOKS
4649-B/21, Ansari Road
Darya Ganj, New Delhi-110 002
Ph.: 23263193/9811582579/09435116718
Fax: 011-23263193
Email: ektabooks@yahoo.com
www.akanshapublishinghouse.com

Subhash Chandra Bose and Fundamental Problems of India

First Published 2012

ISBN 978-93-81763-01-8

[The responsibility for the facts stated, conclusions reached etc., is entirely that of the author. The publishers is not responsible for them, whatsoever.]

PRINTED IN INDIA

Published by Forward Books, New Delhi and Printed at Harmain Offset Press, Delhi.

PREFACE

Rabindranath Tagore (1861-1941) was a deep thinker on race relations and prophet of a new age. On crisis in civilization he wrote, “white other countries were marching ahead, India smothered under the dead weight of British Administration lay static in her helplessness.”

The essays selected for this book contain, political social economic educational issues, concerning India and the world. These problem can be handled successfully by study the wisdom imbibed in this short but timely publications.

Hence by investing in this book Ashutosh Mishra the publishers has earned gratitude and good will of the general readers, policy makers and scholars and students who want to undertake further, indepth studies and research on the subject.

AUTHOR

CONTENTS

1

CRISIS IN CIVILIZATION

Today I complete eighty years of my life. As I turn back to the long stretch of years behind me and view them in clearer perspective, I am struck by the change that has taken place in my attitude and in the psychology of my countrymen, a change that is tragic.

Our direct contact with the wide world of humanity grew out of our link in history with the British race. They came to us with a great literary tradition in which they were truly revealed. The learning we received in those days was meagre and far from diverse; science was still beyond our reach. We learned heavily on English literature—its appreciation became a mark of culture. We endlessly echoed Burke's eloquence and Macaulay's rhetorical strains. We eagerly discussed Shakespeare and Byron and the humanistic political philosophy of the time. True, we were already resolved on gaining our national liberation; but, deep in our hearts, there was a great belief in the liberalism of the British—the vanquished were sure to be led to the path of freedom by the victors themselves. Had not England been an asylum, often, for political refugees, for men who had struggled and suffered in the cause of their country?

This humanism in the British people had our sincere respect. I may add in this context that, during my first visit to Britain in my early youth, I had the chance to listen to John Bright in the House of Parliament as well as outside. His large-hearted radicalism which was far above all nationalist bias made so strong an imprint on my mind that something of it lingers still in these days of sad disillusionment.

Not that the dependence on our rulers' bounty was a matter of pride. This much was commendable, though: we did have the eyes to see intimations of human goodness in an alien race and felt no hesitation in paying it our tribute. The worthiest gifts of human heritage cannot remain the monopoly of a particular land or people; nor do they build a miser's secret hoard that must show no diminution. So it is that English literature, out of which we have gained real sustenance, evokes a response deep within us even today.

It is hard to find an apt Bengali equivalent for the English word "civilization". The civilization of our ancient times was called by Manu *sadachar,* proper conduct. It consisted of a set of conventions which became the social code. Formalism, often unjust, often tyrannical, grew at the expense of freedom of thought. The tenets of conduct which Manu laid down hardened into time-honoured tradition.

In my boyhood the English-educated section of our people felt stirrings of revolt against the rigid social code—the Bengali literature of the time carries portrayals of that revolt. In place of the set code we began to accept the ideal of "civilization" as represented by the English term and illustrated by the British character.

In my own home this change, backed by reason, was warmly greeted and its effect was felt both in theory and practice. Born in such an atmosphere, and impelled by my natural bias towards literature, I saw the British occupying a pedestal of glory.

That early period of my life ended in an agony of disenchantment. I started to discover more and more how those who professed the highest civilized values could cast them aside with the utmost ease, whenever their national interests were at stake.

The moment came when I had to pull myself away from preoccupation with literature. For, the sight of the terrible poverty of the Indian masses grew inescapable, I realized that perhaps in no other modern state was there such a complete denial of the basic needs of living: food and clothing, education and health services. And yet it was the exploited resources of this country that had been adding, year on year, to the wealth of the British race.

Lost in the glamorous aspects of British culture, I had never thought that, out of it could come so cruel a distortion of long cherished values; that distortion, I knew at last, was the emblem of a civilized nation's contempt and callousness towards our vast masses.

This helpless country has been denied mastery over the machine, by means of which the British have strutted as a world power. Meanwhile, through these years, Japan has been using that mastery for a rapid expansion of her economy. I have seen with my own eyes the extent of Japan's prosperity and national uplift. I have witnessed, again, in Moscow the tireless energy with which the Russians have tried to wipe out from their country disease and illiteracy, ignorance, penury and every outward mark of shame. Free from racial prejudice, the Soviets have projected all over their domain the power of human fellowship. The swift and surprising progress they have attained makes me at once happy and jealous!

One unusual aspect of Soviet life that impressed me in Moscow was that the tie of common interests resulted in a great joint endeavour and prevented communal differences from developing into political conflict. Today there are in the world two great Powers, the British and the Russians, who dominate a large number of nationalities. The British have trampled on the manhood of the subject races under their rule, keeping them in a moribund state. It is otherwise in Soviet Russia which has political attachments with many Muslim tribes in its territory. The Government have striven hard and unceasingly for the welfare of those peoples, trying to harmonize the interests of all.

I have also seen Iran, long squeezed between the grindstones of two European Powers, now liberated and working to fulfil her destiny. During my recent visit there I discovered to my delight that the Zoroastrians, once at the mercy of the major community, no longer suffered from repression. Iran's new life started from the time she freed herself from the entanglements of European diplomacy. With all my heart I wish Iran well.

Turning to a neighbouring state, Afghanistan, I find that, while much remains to be done in the fields of education and social development, there are real prospects of continuous progress; for, no European power has yet succeeded in bringing the land of the Afghans into its suffocating grip.

India, however, bearing the immense deadweight of British rule, lies effortless and inert. I recall the tragic history of another country with a great and ancient civilization: China. The British doped the people of China with opium and followed up with territorial aggression. The memory of these happenings had barely dimmed when another outrage came. Japan started to swallow up North China, and that act of brigandage was cynically waved aside by British statesmen as a minor incident. Later, these statesmen lent a crafty hand in wrecking the Republic of Spain.

On the contrary, I saw also how a group of brave Englishmen laid down their lives fighting for freedom in Spain. True, no such generous impulse had stirred in English hearts when an Asian country, China, faced peril; nevertheless, the heroic self-sacrifice in the cause of a European republic vindicated the true English spirit to which in earlier years I had offered homage. And the contrast struck me with renewed force, so that I have to tell this sad story of my gradual loss of faith in the civilization of the West.

Here in India the calamity of civilized rule is apparent not only in the grievous lack of the bare necessaries of life—food, clothing, educational and medical facilities—but even more deplorably in the way the nation has been split, divided against itself. To make matters worse, our social conditions alone are held in blame for the wretched state of affairs, even though this evil could not have taken shape without secret support from the topmost level in the administration.

I do not believe that we Indians are in any way inferior to the Japanese in intellectual calibre. The sharpest contrast in the destinies of the two eastern peoples lies in the fact that, while India has been at the mercy of the British Power, Japan has never suffered from alien domination. We know, indeed, what we have been robbed of. All that the so-called civilized rule has given us is "law and order" and the instruments of a police state. The spirit of liberty has yielded to the display of barefaced might. The withholding of the most precious elements in human relationships has altogether blocked the path of our progress.

And yet it has been my privilege to come in contact with big-hearted Englishmen of surpassing goodness, and it is on account of them that I have not lost faith in the people to whom they belonged. There was Andrews, for instance; in him I had for a very close friend an Englishman, a real Christian and a gentleman. Today, in death's perspective, his complete selflessness and brave magnanimity is all the more luminous. We in India are indebted to Andrews for many acts of love and devotion. But speaking from a personal angle, I am especially grateful to him for this reason: he helped me to regain in my old age some of that sincere respect for the British people which I had acquired in my youth under the power of their literature. The memory of Andrews perpetuates for me the nobility in the British heart. I have counted men like him as my most intimate friends and they are friends of all humanity. To have known such men was for me an enrichment of my life. It is they who will save British honour from shipwreck. At any rate, if I had not seen them and known them, my disillusionment about the peoples of the West would have gone unchallenged.

Meanwhile, the spectre of a new barbarity strides over Europe, teeth bare and claws unconcealed in an orgy of terror. From one end of the Continent to the other the fumes of oppression pollute the atmosphere. The spirit of violence dormant perhaps in the psychology of the West has roused itself and is ready to desecrate the spirit of Man.

The turning of the wheel of fortune will compel the British one day to give up their Indian empire. But what kind of India will they leave behind, what stark misery? When the stream of their two centuries' rule runs dry at last, what a waste of mud and filth will be revealed, bearing a tale of utter futility! There was a time when I used to believe that the springs of a true civilization would issue out of the heart of Europe. Today, as I am about to quit the world, that faith has gone bankrupt.

I live today in the hope that the Saviour is coming, that he will be born in our midst in this poverty-shamed hovel which is India. I shall wait to hear the message he brings with him, the supreme word of promise he speaks unto man from this eastern horizon to give faith and strength to all who hear.

I look back on the stretch of past years and see the crumbling ruins of a proud civilization lying heaped as garbage out of history! And yet I shall not commit the grievous sin of losing faith in Man, accepting his present defeat as final. I shall look forward to a turning in history after the cataclysm is over and the sky is again unburdened and passionless.

Perhaps the new dawn will come from this horizon, from the East where the sun rises; and then, unvanquished Man will retrace his path of conquest, despite all barriers, to win back his lost heritage.

The hour is near when it will be revealed that the insolence of might is fraught with great peril; that hour will bear out in full the truth of what the ancient sages have proclaimed:

Adharmenaidhate tahat tato bhadrani pasyati
Tatah sapatnan jayati samulastu binasyati

By unrighteousness man prospers, gains what seems desirable, defeats enemies, but perishes at the root.

—1941

2

THE CALL OF TRUTH

Parasites have to pay for their ready nutrition by losing the capacity of assimilating food in its natural form. In the history of man the same sin of a capacity allowed to deaden has brought about degeneracy. Man is parasitical not only when he lives on others, but also when he tethers himself inescapably to exterior circumstance, to things as they are and always have been, and drifts, helpless, in the stream. This total surrender to the outward has no sanction from within. When, as a result, man ceases to move by his own volition and is borne by sheer habit, he becomes a kind of parasite. For, he loses the capacity to carry out his assigned task of turning the seemingly impossible into the possible, the way of progress which is his true human destiny.

In this sense the lower animals are all parasites. Carried along by the environment, they live or die by natural selection; they make an advance or get retarded at nature's dictate, and their mind, lacking the power of growth, remains stunted. The bees, for millions of years, could not do anything but shape their hives on one set pattern; thus, while the cells have reached a certain perfection of form, the bees have been victims of the limited and changeless habits of their hive-life. Nature has shown a curious timidity with regard to the lower types of life; she has held them in the protection of her apron strings, and kept their instincts circumscribed lest they stray into bold but dangerous experiments.

Providence, however, displayed a new creative courage when it came to man. His inner nature was set free while outwardly he was weak, naked, defenceless. Exulting in this freedom, man stood up and declared, "I will achieve the impossible. I will not accept the perpetuity of things as they are. I will bring about happenings that have never been before."

So it was that, early in his history, when man found his lot cast among tusked and taloned creatures, he did not seek escape in flight like the deer or in hiding like the tortoise but set himself to work with flints to do the impossible—to make weapons of superior power. The new "tusks and talons" of his were the product of his inner faculties and no gift from nature, and free, therefore, from dependence for their perfection on the caprices of natural selection.

His instruments grew, advancing from flint to iron, proving that his mind was ever questing and not stuck, moribund, to environmental limits. What seemed beyond reach came within his grasp. Not content with the flint ready at hand he knocked at the iron ore under the earth's surface. Not satisfied with the easier process of chipping flints, he proceeded to smelt iron ore and hammer it into shape—what was hardest and most resistant came to be his best support. It is man's nature that he must seek joy, not mere success, in constant action. He must work tirelessly to penetrate from the surface to the depths, from the obvious to the hidden, from the easy to the difficult, from parasitism to free will, from the drive of his passions to the steadiness of self-discipline. That is the way of his conquests.

A group of people put forward the plea: "The flint was the weapon of our revered forefathers; to depart from it is to give up the heritage of our race." So they preserved the heritage of their race, but at the cost of the broader heritage of humanity itself, which also was theirs. We still have people of that kind, existing in the stone age, but they are more outcasts who must hide themselves, as it were, in jungle and cave. Reduced to parasitic living on the environment, yoked blindfold to the drag of things as they are, they who have failed to attain swaraj within themselves must lose it in the outside world too. They lack the awareness that it is man's true function to turn the impossible into the possible by his own prowess; and that he cannot limit himself to what has happened before, but must progress towards what ought to be.

Thirty years ago, when English-educated India was busy begging political rights, I tried to make my countrymen see that man does not have to beg for his rights, he must create them for himself. Man lives by his inner nature and there he is his own master. To depend on gains, from the outside is to hurt one's true self. The denial of our political rights was indeed less grievous than the shameful burden of our prayers and petitions.

Then unrest came upon Bengal under the threat of the knife of Partition. We launched on a boycott of British textiles, but that only helped to swell the profits of mill-owners in Bombay to dizzy figures. I had to say then: "This is not the right way. This is too cheap. All your feelings are directed towards the aliens, and your countrymen are just incidental. Anger gives you all the stimulus, anger against foreigner, and not love for your own people." And I added a warning: "The alien's presence in India is an accident of history; the fact of deeper meaning is that our country is there, that it exists. While one is *maya,* illusion, the other is the inmost reality, the immutable truth. Maya begins to loom large in our view when, either out of anger or out of a warm feeling, we let it become our obsession. Whether we come to grips with it in fury or bow down to it reverently, the result is the same. Maya is like darkness. We cannot cross darkness by means of the fastest steam engine; we cannot wash it away with all the water of the seven oceans. Yet, let the lamp of truth be lit and at its merest flicker maya will vanish. The shastras tell us that even a slight truth rescues us from a vast fear. Fear is a negation in the human mind, it is not to be overcome by another negative; gone for a time, it will find new life and multiply itself over and over again like the monster Raktaveeja. Truth alone has a positive value that will negate negation itself."

Alien government in India is a kind of chameleon. Today it is seen in the guise of the Englishman, tomorrow it may take the form of some other foreigner, and the following day, its malignity unabated, it will bear the semblance of our own countrymen. We may try to hunt down the monster of alien rule with lethal weapons, but it will baffle us every time by changing its skin and complexion. Only when we feel within us that our country exists, that it is real, will the maya recede.

The idea that our homeland is our own just because we have been born in it belongs to those who are fastened, parasitically, to the outer crust of life. Since the true image of man is in his deeper nature, whatever country he helps to create by his wisdom and will, devotion and action, becomes his real homeland. Even the Architect of the universe has to find Himself in His own handiwork!

What precisely do we mean when we speak of creating one's own country? We mean that we spread our inner spirit to the vast outward realm, and apply to it our thought, action and service. A man's homeland has to be a projection as well as mirror of his inmost life.

Years back, in an article entitled *Society and State,* I discussed how we could make the land of our birth truly ours. I underlined the fact that we must win over our country, not from some foreigner but from our own inertia, our indifference. Whenever we have sought boons at the door of the alien government, we have only made our inertia the more intense. The credit for all progress goes to the government, with the effect that our country is increasingly lost to us. We pay out in spiritual values for what we secure as material benefits.

Yagnavalkya has said:

Na va arey putrasya kamaya putrah priyo bhavati

Atmanastu kamaya putrah priyo bhavati.

"The son is dear to us not just because we desire a son but because we seek to realize in him our own self."

This applies also to our homeland; it has to be dear to us, since it is the expression of our own self. When we get that awareness, we shall no longer have to wait on the pleasure of others for our country's constructive progress.

There was nothing in that viewpoint that could have grated in the ears of our patriots, but I cannot forget the storm of protest I roused. It was due to two causes: sheer anger, and avarice.

To give vent to one's wrath is a kind of emotional luxury. There was nothing in those days to stop our revelry of self-indulgence—we went about picketing, burning bales of cloth, admonishing all who did not follow at our heels, with no restraint in language or conduct. Shortly after it was all over, a Japanese friend asked me: "How is it that you people cannot carry on your work with quiet patience and firm resolve? This dissipation of energy is not the best way to try to arrive at one's goal." I had to reply: "If the goal were clear in our view, we would naturally act with restraint; but since we can merely indulge in gestures of wrath, our mounting frenzy, with the purpose lost, throws our energy into reckless waste until nothing of it is left." Anyhow, there were my countrymen, tolerating no check to the exhibition of their outraged feelings. It was all so fantastic! At that point I came to the scene pleading for a different line of action, and succeeded only in drawing some of the wrath on to my own head.

Then, the question of avarice. Worth-while objects have always been attained only the hard way. We, however, hit upon a device to get them cheap—begging, not with folded hands, but in a tone that carried a threat. The country was overjoyed at the ingenuity of this trick. It was like being at a reduced price sale—goods in the political market were marked at cut rates. He whose means are slender gets so taken up with low prices that he pays no heed to quality and rushes to attack anyone who has doubts in that respect.

The outer appearance, maya, possessed us in those days. Significantly, a political leader of the time said, "I have one hand at the throat of the British Government and the other at its feet." So he had no hand left for his country! That attitude has changed since. We now have one party that has both its hands at the alien government's throat while the hands of another are down at its feet. Neither gesture can help, though. No gestures concerned merely with the foreigner can help.

In those days the stimulus from every side was directed at the heart of Bengal. But emotion by itself, like fire, only consumes its fuel, which it reduces to ashes—it has no creative power. The mind of man must be at work with patience, skill and foresight, employing this fire to melt the hard materials at hand and make them malleable. We failed to rouse our intellectual forces, and so we could not build any organization of permanent worth out of the vast, flaming emotion of the time.

The cause of our failure was within ourselves. For a long time past all our actions had been dominated by emotion on the one hand and habit on the other. Our power of thought had remained dormant, we dared not give it free play. So, when we had to be roused to action, it was our emotion which was requisitioned in a hurry and the hypnotism of some mystical formula was applied to our intellect.

With this deadening of the mind, delusion comes easy and any promise of an Aladdin's lamp makes the greedladen heart throb. It must be admitted that there is nothing to beat Aladdin's lamp, if only we could have it. However, the man whose greed is great and capacity feeble would not admit this. A mere promise of the lamp would rouse him to eager exertion; and to point out the futility of his hopes would make him yell hard, as though he were being robbed of all his property.

In the excitement of the Partition days a band of youths sought to bring about the millennium by revolution. They cast themselves as a sacrifice into the fire they had lighted and, on that account, deserve salutation not from us alone but from all the world. Even their failure carries the radiance of spiritual glory. Through supreme self-dedication and travail they had to realize at last that when the country was not ready, the path of revolution led nowhere. The false track which had seemed a short cut to the goal did not reach it and thorns and brambles tore at the marching feet. To pay part price for a thing may lose both the price and the thing. The daring youths of those days had thought that the sacrifice of their lives on behalf of all the people would bring about a revolution. They paid the highest price in their power but it was not enough. The deliverance of a people must spring out of all their hearts, not from the heart of a section. On a railway train a first-class compartment with all its rich fittings cannot go faster than the third-class coaches attached to it. I feel sure that the survivors in that patriotic band have now realized that the country has to be the creation of all its people, a concrete expression of mass mind and will, every faculty pressed into full use.

When we turn our gaze upon the progress of other nations, the political cart-horse comes prominently into view—on it seems to depend wholly the speed of the vehicle. We forget that the cart behind the horse must also be in a fit state to move; its wheels must have the right alignment, its parts must have been properly assembled. The cart is the product not simply of materials on which saw and hammer had worked; thought, energy and application have gone into its making. We have seen countries that are outwardly free, but as they are drawn by the horse of politics the rattle rouses all the neighbourhood from sleep and the jolting makes the limbs of the passengers ache; the vehicles break down repeatedly on their way and to put them in running order is a terrific business. Yet they are vehicles of a sort, after all. The fragments that pass for our country not only lack cohesion but are comprised of parts at odds with one another. To hitch it to anger or avarice or some other passion, drag it along painfully with much din and bustle, and call this political progress! How long could the driving force last? Is it not wiser, then, to keep the horse in the stable for the time and take up the task, first, of putting the vehicle in good shape?

It appears from the writings of the young men of Bengal who have turned back from the portals of death that such thoughts are troubling their minds too. They say that what we need above all else is self-preparation, a striving to develop the inner man, so that the groundwork for a common endeavour may be ready. This has to be achieved not by blind obedience to an external bidding but by disciplined reason. Whatever fails to illumine the mind and keeps the mind in a state of daze, is a deterrent.

To make the country our own by means of our creative power is indeed a great call. It cannot be a mere summons to some mechanical exercise. For, man does not limit himself in the manner of the bee building endless replicas of cells, or the spider weaving webs of one pattern. His greatest strength is within him and it is up to him to draw on that strength and not on blind habit. To tell him, "Do not think but act," is to help prolong the age-old delusion that has held this country in its deadly grip. We have been content much too long to surrender our greatest right—the right to reason and decide for ourselves—to the blind forces of sacred injunctions and established habit. We have said: "We must not cross the black water; it is forbidden by Manu. We cannot partake of a meal with a Muslim; it is against prescribed usage." In other words, we have pursued a routine of habit in which the mind has no place. We have thus been reduced to the helpless condition of the master who is entirely dependent on his servant. The real master, I repeat, is the man within; he gets into endless trouble when he ties himself down to outward circumstance, a parasite, an automaton built in the workshop of sheer servility. The inertia from which our slave mentality has grown could hardly be broken by a further dose of blindfold submission, or the imposition of the motions of a wound-up mechanical doll.

The movement which has now succeeded the struggle against Partition is far greater in size and has spread all over India. Previously, the vision of our political leaders had never gone beyond the English-educated classes—they alone had counted. The country was a mirage formed of vapourings in the English language, in which flitted about the thin shades of Burke and Gladstone, Mazzini and Garibaldi. No spirit of sacrifice was involved, no true compassion for the people. Then, at the crucial moment, Mahatma Gandhi came and stood at the door of India's destitute millions, clad as one of themselves, speaking to them in their own language. It was a real happening, not a tale on the printed page. That is why he has been so aptly named Mahatma, Great Soul. Who else has so unreservedly accepted the vast masses of the Indian people as his own flesh and blood? At the touch of truth the pent-up forces of the spirit are set free. As soon as love stood at India's door, it flew open. All inward niggardliness was gone. Truth awakened truth.

Stratagem in politics is a barren policy—that was a lesson of which we were sorely in need. All honour to the Mahatma, who wakened us to the power of truth. But the cowardly and the weak take easily to cheap tactics. Even today our worldly-wise ones have not been rid of the idea of using the Mahatma as a disguised and ingenious move in their political gamble. Minds corrupted by untruth cannot grasp the meaning of the great love kindled in the people's heart by the Mahatma's love.

This, indeed, is the birth of freedom, nothing less. It is the country's discovery of itself. It has little to do with the alien occupation of India. This love is pure affirmation. It does not involve itself in arguments with the negative attitude. There is no need for arguments of any kind whatever.

Some notes of the music of this wonderful awakening of India by the call of love radiated across the seas and reached me abroad. What joy it was to think we would all be summoned to witness the great arousal in which the splendid power latent in India's heart was to find full release. This, I did believe, was real liberation. When the Buddha proclaimed his doctrine of compassion for all living beings, the stimulus of the ideal touched every aspect of life and enriched the creative arts: in that distant age, too, India had been cracking up repeatedly in spite of sporadic attempts at political unity. The stimulus was so strong that it reached out even beyond the Indian borders and made people in many countries conscious of their inner wealth. No great conqueror or merchant prince could ever achieve anything of this kind—they merely carried with them discord and pain and insult. Love attains its object of redemption by touching life at its taproot, while avarice has to use the instruments of coercion. This we had noticed during the anti-Partition struggle, when men often made sacrifices under the outward pressure of avarice, not the inner compulsion of love. Avarice has to get quick results, even if they are impermanent; the fruit of love is durable and it is sufficient by itself.

So, in the excited expectation or breathing the air of a new-found freedom, I hurried back to my homeland. But what I have seen and felt troubles me. Something seems to be weighing on the people's spirit; a stern pressure is at work; it makes everyone talk in the same voice and make the same gestures.

When I wanted to ask questions and decide for myself, my well-wishers clapped anxious hands to my mouth: "Pray be silent." There is a tyranny in the air—even if intangible, it is worse than open violence. Let anyone who doubts the wisdom of the proclaimed policy speak his mind in a bare whisper, and he will have to face disciplinary action. One of our newspapers dared give a mere hint of disapproval of the burning of foreign cloth, and the readers' agitated protest came menacingly; the flames which had consumed the bales of mill cloth could quickly reduce this paper to ashes!

I see a section of the people fanatically engaged in their assigned task, and another section struck with alarm and dumbfounded. The idea prevails that all questioning must stop; there should be nothing but blind obedience. Obedience to whom? To some charmed words of incantation, to some reasonless creed!

And why this obedience? Here again is avarice, our spiritual foe. The country has been given a very attractive promise—it is to have in no time a treasure of inestimable worth. Under its lure men have cast reason aside and are full of resentment against all who will not behave like-wise. The sadness is that, even those who have not swallowed the bait are anxious to make use of it. "It will serve a good purpose," they say. They evidently think that the India that declared, "In truth alone is victory, in naught else *(satyameba jayate nanritam)*" is unfit for self-government.

To make matters worse, the gain which is envisaged has a name but it is not defined. Even as a fear which is vague is all the more terrifying, the haziness of a lure makes it all the more tempting. Left to the imagination, everyone can give it a form according to his preference. An attempt to inquire into its real nature is of no avail, for it can easily camouflage itself. Thus, while the temptation has been magnified by its indefiniteness, the means of attainment and the hour have been precisely indicated. Many people are convinced that self-government will be won on a certain date of a certain month close ahead. Having given up their freedom of mind, they deprive others of that freedom. It is as if we have been seeking an exorcist to drive out a ghost, and then the ghost itself turns up in the guise of the exorcist.

The Mahatma has captured the heart of India with his love; we all bow down to him on that account. He has revealed to us the full power of truth and for that we are beholden. We read about eternal truths in books, we talk about them, but it is a propitious moment when we encounter truth face to face. Such an opportunity is rare in one's life. It is easy enough to go from province to province making political speeches, and even to make and break National Congresses.

But the golden wand of true love that has wakened us out of age-long slumber is not to be easily found. To the possessor of that rare wand, our profound salutation.

But then, what is the good of it all if, even after we have seen the face of truth, our faith in it is not firm enough? Our minds must accept the truth of the intellect just as the heart accepts the truth of love. Till now, neither the Congress nor any other institution made a strong impression on the heart of India—it needed the touch of love. Now that we have the truth of love, are we to withdraw our trust in the other truth—just where swaraj is concerned?

Let me give an illustration. I am looking for a *veena* player. I have tried everywhere but failed to find the right man. They are all experts, they command high fees, but their technical skill draws my admiration without touching my emotions. At last I find a player whose very first notes are sheer rhapsody. I accept him as my master. I then want a veena made, but my resources turn out to be inadequate. What if the master, pitying my plight, says, "Do not worry. Take this stick, tie a string down its length, and practise on that contraption. On a particular day of a particular month the stick will turn into a real veena." Would that help? It would in fact be mistaken kindness for the master thus to take pity on my circumstances. Far better, if he were to tell me that such things could not be had cheaply; that a real veena could not be made with a single string; that it needed a great variety of materials and skilled craftsmanship; that a single slip would result in its being out of tune.

Let our faith in the Mahatma's capacity for love never diminish; but swaraj is not a matter of a stick and a single string. It is a vast enterprise involving complex processes and needing as much study and clear thinking as impulse and emotion. Economists and educationists and mechanical engineers must contribute their ideas and exertions to the pool of this manysided endeavour. The intellect of the people must be fully awake, so that the spirit of inquiry is untramelled; minds must not be overawed or made inactive by compulsions, open or secret.

It is not any or every call to which the country responds—we know that from past experience. Since no one has yet been able to unite the country's forces in this creative task, time has gone to waste. And we have waited for him who has the right and the power to make the call on us. Once, in the forest hermitage, our gurus in the fullness of their knowledge and wisdom had sent forth such a call:

> *Yathapa prabatayanti yatha masa aharjaram*
> *Ebang mang brahmacharino dhata ayantu*
> *sarbata swaha*

> "As the streams take a downward course, as the months move on to the year, so let all brahmacharis come to me from every direction."

The true vision of that ancient age lives on; its voice flings echoes. Then, why should not our supreme leader of today send his summons likewise, rallying the people's full capacity for action? Why should he not say, "Let all who hear me come from every direction?" Freedom lies in the complete arousal of the people. God has given the Mahatma the voice that can call. Why should this not be our supreme moment?

His call has come, but only to a restricted field. To one and all he has simply said, "Spin and weave, spin and weave." Is this the strident call of the new age for a vast striving? When nature summoned the bee to a narrow hive-life, millions of bees responded and made themselves sexless for the sake of efficiency. But this sacrifice by way of self-atrophy led to the opposite of freedom. People who do not hesitate to neutralize their power in answer to some command carry within them their prison-cell. The call to the easy way is for the bee, not for man. Man reveals himself in all his strength only when his utmost capacity is demanded.

Sparta tried to become strong by harnessing her manpower on a restricted field, but she could not attain her purpose. Athens, on the contrary, sought to give full play to all the capacities of her people and she did win—the banner of her victory still stands unfurled on the crest of civilization. The stature of man is getting stunted systematically in the factories and barracks of Europe; humanity stands sacrificed to narrow self-interest. Is that not the reason why the darkness of misery thickens in the West? Man could be dwarfed by machines both big and small—by massive engines and the petty spinning-wheel. That wheel in its right place would surely do good. But where, owing to the diversity in man's temperament, the *charka* is misplaced, the thread is spun at the cost of something in the mind itself. The mind, surely, is not of less account than a length of cotton thread spun on the wheel!

It has been argued that four-fifths of the Indian people are engaged in cultivation and for half the year they remain unemployed; to set an example to them, people of the higher classes should take to the charka for a time. But, to start with, the basic assumptions have to be proved. How many cultivators become workless, and for how long? Would they earn more by spinning than by other means? It is also open to doubt whether it would be good to offer all the peasantry just one other means of livelihood apart from cultivation. In a word, we should not be prepared to formulate a general policy by sheer guesswork. We demand research on scientific lines; when that is done, it will be time to draw conclusions.

I hear the voice of protest: "We do not propose to curb the mind for ever, but only for a short while." Why, even for a short while? Is it because that brief period will be enough for us to gain swaraj? That does not make sense. Swaraj is not a matter of mere self-sufficiency in the production of cloth. Its real place is within us—the mind with its diverse power goes on building swaraj for itself. Nowhere in the world has this work been completed; in some part of the body-politic a lingering greed or delusion keeps up the bondage. And that bondage is always within the mind itself.

As everywhere else, swaraj in this country has to find its basis in the mind's unfoldment, in knowledge, in scientific thinking, and not in shallow gestures. It does not make sense to say that we could attain this swaraj by plying the spinning-wheel a brief while. If we agree to accept oracular prophecies from human lips, there will be an addition to our thousand-and-one superstitions. As soon as it appears that nothing but oracles serve to move us, they will have to be manufactured day and night out of sheer necessity, and all other voices will then be hushed. As dogma takes the place of reason, freedom will give way to some kind of despotism. This is not a new thing. We in India have enough of the supernatural—mystical revelations, magical healing, and all sorts of divine intervention in the affairs of the world. That is just why I am so anxious to reinstate reason on its lost pedestal.

There is the bonfire of heaped mill cloth, before the very eyes of the Mother deep in shame because of her nakedness. I see no urgency for such waste except in the power of a superstition. The question of using or boycotting British-made cloth is one for economists to decide. In discussing it, the language of economics must be employed. If people cannot think scientifically, our very first battle should be against that sad state of mind. Such incapacity is the original sin out of which all other ills flow. That original sin finds support when it is proclaimed that foreign cloth is "impure" and deserves to be destroyed. Economics is tossed aside for the falsehood passing as a moral dictum.

Untruth itself is impure and is to be shunned, and not simply on the ground that it fails to serve our purpose. Whatever its other effects, it makes our inner nature unclean; that is a moral premise above the plane of economics or politics. Besides, if there is anything wrong in using cloth of a particular brand, the offence would be against economics or hygiene or aesthetics, but certainly not against ethics. The counter-argument goes that any error that brings about sorrow is a moral wrong. To that I answer that sorrow follows in the trail of every error. An error in geometry will make a road too long, or a foundation weak, or a bridge dangerous. But mathematical errors cannot be corrected by ethics. If a student stumbles in his geometry problem, it will do no good to tear up his exercise book—the problem will have to be worked anew by the right geometrical method. What if the schoolmaster concludes that unless the exercise book itself is destroyed the boy will not be convinced of his error? If this is right, I can only say that the boy needs reformation much more than academic lessons.

We have been ordered to burn foreign cloth. I, for one, am unable to obey. First, because I believe it to be my duty to fight the habit of blind obedience. Secondly, I feel that the cloth to be burnt is not mine, it belongs to people who are sorely in need of it. We who seem to be doing an act of sacrifice through this incendiarism have other sources of supply; but those who are really hit cannot stir out of doors because of their nakedness. Forced atonement will not wash off our sins; nor will the gain of some apparent benefits make up for the loss of the reasoned will.

The Mahatma has declared war against the tyranny of the machine which is oppressing the world. Here we are all under his banner. But we cannot accept as our ally in the fight the slave mentality that is at the root of all the misery and indignity in our national life. That, indeed, is our real enemy and through its defeat alone can swaraj within and without come to us.

I am ready to burn cloth, but not under the blind pressure of a directive. Let experts give this question their time and thought and convince us with arguments what economic means could cure the economic malady arising from our use of foreign cloth. If we have committed an economic crime by using a certain make of cloth, how could we be sure, in the absence of logical data, that by burning cloth we would not simply broaden the basis of the crime, so that the stranglehold of Manchester would strengthen all the more? I am not speaking as an expert, since I am not one; I am only asking a question out of the spirit of inquiry. Not that I accept as gospel truth whatever the experts say. But, then, they do not speak in the idiom of gospels; they make a call on our intelligence and urge us to frank debate.

It is time for us today to consider another point. India's awakening is a part of the awakening of the world. With the Great War the door of a new age has flung open. The peoples of the earth have been drawing closer to one another, almost unawares; but as all humanity feels the stress of war, the fact of their mutual dependence can no longer be denied. All at once the foundations of civilization, western civilization to be precise, seem to quake. It is evident that the tremors are neither local nor momentary; they are worldwide and will not stop until human relationships, reaching from continent to continent, become based on true harmony.

Henceforth, any nation which seeks isolation for itself must come into conflict with the time-spirit and find no peace. From now onward the plane of thinking of every nation will have to be international. It is the striving of the new age to develop in the mind this faculty of universality. Of late we have noted a change in the basic policies of our Indian administration. There is an attempt to see the problems of India against the framework of the world. The war has lifted a veil that used to limit our mental vision: what is contrary to the interests of the world at large is against our interests too—that maxim, long confined to the printed word, is now visible in practice. Mankind has understood that the rights of possession, wrongfully won, are not valid; that it is a gain rather than a loss to sacrifice some apparent rights for the reality itself. This far-reaching change in outlook is leading the mind of man from the petty to the great and it is helping to transform Indian politics. There are hindrances to be overcome—self-interest attacks enlightened understanding at every step. But, then, it would be wrong to think that self-interest alone is genuine.

In my sixty years' experience I have discovered that pure hypocrisy is not easy to attain and is a scarce commodity. The out-and-out hypocrite is a rare phenomenon. The fact is that every man is more or less ambivalent in character. But our logical faculty is unable to admit the two opposites together. When we see the good along with the bad, we rush to the conclusion that the good is counterfeit. In international relations this duality is clear. We are apt to be obsessed by this aspect in view of all our past experience; but in the light of future promise, we must accept the change in outlook as genuine. The urge of the future age, which we feel even today, is towards the unity of man. The establishment of the League of Nations and the Indian Constitutional reforms—they are messages from the West pointing to the future. Even if the messages do not fully reveal the truth, they strain in all sincerity towards the truth.

At this dawn of the world's awakening, if our own national endeavour holds no intimations of a universal message, the poverty of our spirit will be laid piteously bare. I do not say that we should neglect the immediate tasks we have in hand. But when the bird is roused at daybreak, all its awakening is not absorbed in the quest for food: its wings respond to the call of the sky and its throat pours forth joyous songs in celebration of the new light. Universal humanity has sent us its urgent call. Let our mind answer in its own language. Formerly, we were engrossed in discovering and pointing out the faults and shortcomings of our rulers. Now that we are bent on dissociating our politics from dependence, are we to continue that recital to feed our policy of boycott? The dust of angry passion will only obscure the greater world from our view. And we shall exhibit a sorry image of our country if we fail to see for ourselves the vast dimensions of India in its world context.

Regrettably, we have narrowed down our vision to mere material expectations. But even in the West a real concern to rise superior to material interests is now apparent. There I have come across men in whom the new spirit of renunciation is personified. Those are men who, freed of the petty bonds of nationalism, feel within them the inner oneness of all mankind, and are ready for every sacrifice in working for the fulfilment of the great ideal. I have seen such men in England; they have accepted insult and hurt from the hands of their own people in their struggle to liberate subject races from the tyranny of power. I have seen such renunciation in

France too—there is Romain Rolland, for instance, an outcast among his countrymen. I have also seen this in the minor States of Europe. I have watched the faces of students in Europe, radiant with the hope of world unity, and bearing with patience and courage the blows they must suffer for their dream of the glorious age ahead.

In this propitious dawn, are we alone to harp on the faults of others and base our constructive programmes on ill feelings? In this new dawn shall we not remember Him, who is one *(Ya ekah),* who is without distinction of colour *(avarnah)* and who with His multiple power makes true provision for the inherent needs of each and every class *(Vahudhashakti yogat varnananekan nihitartho dadhati)?* Shall we not pray to the Giver of wisdom to unite us all in right understanding *(sa no buddhya subhaya samyunantu)?*

—1921

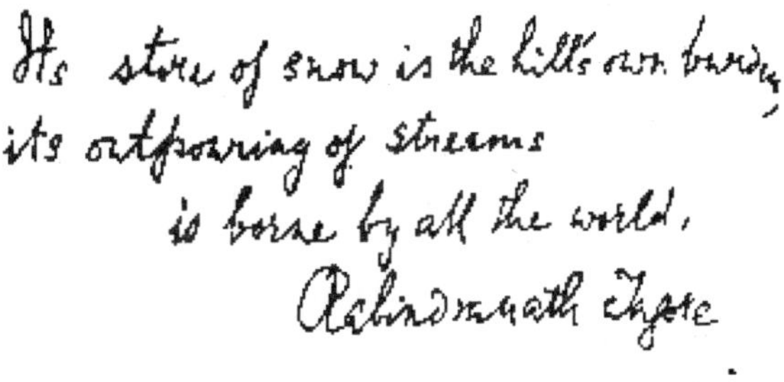

3

A POET'S SCHOOL

From questions that have often been put to me, I have come to feel that the public claims an apology from the poet for having founded a school, as I in my rashness have done. One must admit that the silkworm which spins and the butterfly that floats on the air represent two different stages of existence, contrary to each other. The silkworm seems to have a cash value credited in its favour somewhere in Nature's accounting department, according to the amount of work it performs. But the butterfly is irresponsible. The significance which it may possess has neither weight nor use and is lightly carried on its pair of dancing wings. Perhaps it pleases someone in the heart of the sunlight, the Lord of colours, who has nothing to do with account books and has a perfect mastery in the great art of wastefulness.

The poet may be compared to that foolish butterfly. He also tries to translate in verse the festive colours of creation. Then why should he imprison himself in duty? Why should he make himself accountable to those who would assess his produce by the amount of profit it would earn?

I suppose this poet's answer would be that, when he brought together a few boys, one sunny day in winter, among the warm shadows of the tall straight *sal* trees with their branches of quiet dignity, he started to write a poem in a medium not of words.

In these self-conscious days of psycho-analysis clever minds have discovered the secret spring of poetry in some obscure stratum of repressed freedom, in some constant fretfulness of thwarted self-realization. Evidently in this instance they were right. The phantom of my long-ago boyhood did come to haunt its early beginning; it sought to live in the lives of other boys, and to build its missing paradise with ingredients which may not have any orthodox material, prescribed measure, or standard value.

This brings to my mind Kalidasa, a poet of ancient India. Happily for the scholars, Kalidasa, has left behind him no clear indication of his birth-place, and there is ample scope for endless disagreement. My scholarship does not pretend to go deep, but I remember having read somewhere that he was born in beautiful Kashmir. Since then I have given up reading discussions about his birth-place lest I find some learned contradiction equally convincing. Anyhow, it is in the fitness of things that Kalidasa should have been born in Kashmir—and I envy him, for I was born in Calcutta.

But psycho-analysis need not be disappointed, for he was banished to a city in the plains and *Meghaduta* vibrates with the music of sorrow that has its keynote "in the remembrance of happier things." It is significant that in this poem the lover's errant fancy, in quest of the beloved who dwelt in the paradise of eternal beauty, lingered with enjoyment about every hill, stream, or forest over which it passed; watched the grateful dark eyes of the peasant girls welcoming the rain-laden clouds of June; listened to some village elder reciting under the banyan tree a familiar love legend fresh with the tears and smiles of simple-souled generations. We feel in all this the prisoner of the stony-hearted city revelling in a vision of joy that, in his imaginary journey, followed him from hill to hill, waited at every turn of the path which bore the finger-posts of heaven for separated lovers banished on the earth.

It was not a physical home-sickness from which the poet suffered, it was something far more fundamental—the nostalgia of the soul. We feel in almost all his works the oppressive atmosphere of the King's palaces of those days, thick with luxury and the callousness of self-indulgence, and yet an atmosphere of refined culture, of an extravagant civilization.

The poet in the royal court lived in exile, as it were. It was, he knew, not merely his own exile but that of the whole age to which he was born, the age that had amassed wealth and well-being, and lost its background of the great universe. What was the image in which his desire of perfection persistently appeared in his poems and dramas? It was tapovana, the forest resort of the patriarchal community of ancient India. Those who are familiar with Sanskrit literature know that this was not a colony of people with a primitive culture. They were seekers of truth, for the sake of which they lived in purity but not puritanism; they led a simple life, but not one of self-mortification. They did not advocate celibacy and were in close touch with people who pursued worldly interests. Their aim was briefly suggested in the Upanishad in these lines:

Te sarvagam sarvatah prapya dhira
Yuktatmanah sarvamevavisanti.

Those men of serene mind enter into the All,
having realized and being everywhere in union
with the omnipresent Spirit.

It was no negative philosophy of renunciation. Kalidasa, living in the prosperous city of Ujjaini in the glorious days of Vikramditya, his mind oppressed by material objects and by its own demands, let his thoughts escape to the vision of tapovana, and into life, light and freedom.

It was no deliberate copying but natural coincidence, that a poet of modern India should have a like vision when he felt within him the misery of a spiritual exile. In Kalidasa's time the people strongly believed in the ideal of tapovana, the forest colony, and there can be no doubt that even in that late age there were communities of men living in the heart of nature—not ascetics intent on a slow suicide but men of serene intellect who sought to realize the inward meaning of their life. When Kalidasa sang of the topovana, his verses instantly touched the living faith of his listeners. But today the idea of the tapovana has lost all semblance with reality and has slipped into legend; therefore, in a modern poem, it would merely be "literary". Then again, the tapovana concept would be a fantastic anachronism in the present age, unless recast under the current conditions of life. That, indeed, was the reason why the poet of today had to compose his verse in a plausible language.

But I must give that history in some detail.

Civilized man has come far away from the orbit of his normal life. He has gradually formed and intensified some habits, like those of the bees, for adapting himself to his hive-world. We so often see modern men suffering from world-weariness, from a sense of revolt against their environment. Social revolutions are ushered in with a suicidal violence that is rooted in our dissatisfaction with our hive-wall arrangement—the too exclusive enclosure that deprives us of the perspective needed in our art of living. All this is an indication that man has not really been moulded in the model of the bee, and therefore he becomes recklessly anti-social when his freedom to be more than social is ignored.

In our highly complex modern conditions, mechanical forces are organized with such efficiency that the materials produced grow far in advance of man's capacity to select and assimilate them to suit his nature and needs. Such an overgrowth, like the rank vegetation of the tropics, creates confinement for man. The nest is simple. It has an easy relationship with the sky; the cage is complex and costly, it is too much itself, excommunicating whatever lies outside. And modem man is busy building his cage. He is always occupied in adapting himself to its dead angularities, limiting himself to its limitations, and so he becomes a part of it.

This talk may seem too oriental to some of my listeners. I am told that they believe in a constant high pressure of living produced by an artificially cultivated hunger for material objects. This according to them generates and feeds the energy driving civilization upon its endless journey. Personally, I do not believe that this has ever been the main driving force behind any great civilization. But I have touched on this theme in order to explain the conduct of a poet trespassing into a region reserved for experts and for those who have academic distinction.

I was born in what was then the metropolis of British India. Our ancestors came floating to Calcutta upon the earliest tide of the fluctuating fortune of the East India Company. The code of life for our family became composed of three cultures, Hindu, Muslim, and British. My grandfather belonged to that period when an extravagance in dress and courtesy and a generous leisure were gradually being clipped and curtailed into Victorian manners. I came to a world in which the modern city-bred spirit of progress had just triumphed over the lush green life of our ancient village community.

Though the trampling process was almost complete around me, something of the past lingered over the wreckage. In my boyhood days I often listened to my eldest brother dwelling regretfully on a society that had been hospitable, kindly, and filled with a simple faith and the ceremonial poetry of life. All that was a vanishing shadow in the twilight haze of the horizon; the all-pervading fact was the modern city, newly built by a Company of western traders, and the spirit of the new times striking upon our life, even if it had to face countless anomalies. But it has always been a surprise to me that while this hard crust of a city was my only experience of the world, I was constantly haunted by the nostalgic fancies of an exile.

It seems that the sub-conscious remembrance of some primeval dwelling-place, where in our ancestors' minds were figured and voiced the mysteries of the inarticulate rocks, the rushing water and the dark whispers of the forest, was constantly stirring my blood with its call. (Some living memory in me seemed to ache for the play-ground it had once shared with the primal life in the illimitable magic of land, water and air.) The thin, shrill cry of the high-flying kite in the blazing sun of a dazed Indian midday sent to a solitary boy the signal of a dumb distant kinship. The few cocoanut palms growing by the boundary wall of our house, like some war captives from an older army of invaders of this earth, spoke to me of the eternal companionship which the great brotherhood of trees have ever offered to man. They made my heart thrill to the invitation of the forest. I had the good fortune of answering this invitation when as a boy of ten I stood alone on the Himalayas under the shade of great *deodars,* awed by the dark dignity of life's first-born aristocracy, by its sturdy fortitude that was terrible as well as courteous.

Looking back upon those moments of my boyhood when all my mind seemed to float poised upon a large feeling of the sky, of the light, I cannot help believing that my Indian ancestry has left deep in my being the legacy of its philosophy, the philosophy which speaks of fulfilment through harmony with nature. It arouses in us a great desire to seek our freedom, not in the man-made world but in the depth of the universe; and it makes us offer our reverence to the divinity inherent in fire, water and trees, in everything moving and growing. The founding of my school had its origin in the memory of that longing for freedom, the memory which seems to go back beyond the sky-line of my birth.

Freedom in the mere sense of independence is meaningless. Perfect freedom lies in the harmony of relationship which we realize not through *knowing,* but in *being.* Objects of knowledge maintain an infinite distance from us who are the knowers. For knowledge is not union. We attain the world of freedom only through perfect sympathy.

Children with the freshness of their senses come directly to the intimacy of this world. This is the first great gift they have. They must accept it naked and simple and never lose their power of quick communication. For our perfection we have to be at once savage and civilized; we must be natural with nature and human with human society. The misery which I felt was due to the crowded solitude in which I dwelt in a city where man was everywhere, with no gap for the immense non-human. My banished soul, in the isolation of town-life, cried within me for new horizons. I was like the torn-away line of a verse, always in a state of suspense, the other line with which it rhymed and which could give it fullness, having been smudged. The easy power to be happy which, along with other children, I brought with me to this world, was being constantly worn away by friction with the brick-and-mortar arrangement of life, the mechanical habits and the customary code of respectability.

In the usual course I was sent to school, but possibly my suffering was unusual, greater than that of most other children. The non-civilized in me was sensitive; it had a great thirst for colour, for music, for the movements of life. Our city-built education took no heed of that living fact. It had its luggage-van waiting for branded bales of marketable result. The non-civilized and the civilized in man should be in the same proportion as water and land on our globe, the former predominating. But the school had for its object a continual reclamation of the non-civilized. Such a drain of the living water causes an aridity which may not be considered deplorable in a city, but my nature never became accustomed to those conditions. The non-civilized triumphed in me too soon and drove me away from school when I had just entered my teens. I found myself stranded on a solitary island of ignorance and had to rely solely on my own instincts to build up my education from the very beginning.

This reminds me that when I was young I had the great good fortune of coming upon a Bengali translation of Robinson Crusoe. I still believe that it is one of the best books for boys ever written. I have already spoken in this paper about my longing when young to run away from my own self and be one with everything in nature. I have described this mood as particularly Indian, the outcome of traditional desire for the expansion of consciousness. One has to admit that such a desire is too subjective, but this is inevitable in our geographical circumstances. We live under the tyranny of the tropics, paying heavy toll every moment for the barest right of existence. The heat, the damp, the unspeakable fecundity of minute life feeding upon big life, the perpetual sources of irritation, visible and invisible, leave little margin of capital for extravagant experiments.

Excess of energy seeks obstacles to fight with and overcome. That is why we find so often in western literature a constant emphasis on the malignant aspect of Nature; in her the people of the West discover an enemy, for the sheer pleasure of challenging her to fight. The same reason which made Alexander wish for other worlds to conquer when his conquest of this world was complete made these enormously vital people go out of their way and spread their coat-tails in other peoples' thoroughfares, claiming indemnity when these are trodden upon. To enjoy the risk of hurting themselves they are ready to hurt others who are inoffensive; the birds which know how to fly away, the timid beasts which inhabit inaccessible regions, and... I shall avoid the discourtesy of mentioning higher races.

Life needs hurdles on its path for its advance. The stream would lose the speed of its flow without the resistance of the soil through which it must cut its way. The spirit of combat is part of the genius of life. The tuning of an instrument helps music to be perfectly realized. Let us rejoice that, in the West, life's instrument is being tuned in all its chords through the contest with obstacles. The creativeness in the heart of the universe will never let obstacles be completely removed. It is only because there is an ideal of perfection to attain that the spirit of combat is great.

In Robinson Crusoe, the delight in union with nature finds its expression in a story of adventure where the solitary man is face to face with solitary nature, coaxing her, co-operating with her, exploring her secrets, using all his faculties to win her help. The pleasure I felt in reading this book was not in sharing the pride of human success against the closed fist of a parsimonious nature, but in the harmony with nature attained through intelligent dealings. And this is the heroic love-adventure of the West, the active wooing of the earth.

I remember how in my youth, in the course of a railway journey across Europe from Brindisi to Calais, I watched with keen delight and wonder that continent glowing with richness under the age-long attention of her chivalrous lover, western humanity. He had gained her, made her his own, unlocked the inexhaustible generosity of her heart. And I had intently wished that the introspective vision of the universal soul which an eastern devotee experiences in the solitude of his mind could be united with this spirit of service.

I remember a morning when a beggar woman in a Bengal village gathered in the loose end of her sari the stale flowers that were about to be thrown away from the vase on my table; and with a look of ecstatic tenderness she buried her face in them, exclaiming, "Beloved of my heart!" Her eyes could easily pierce the veil of the outward form and reach the realm of the infinite in these flowers where she found the intimate touch of her beloved. But in spite of it all she lacked that energy of worship, the western form of direct divine service, which helps the earth to bring out her flowers and spread the reign of beauty on the desolate dust. I refuse to think that the twin spirits of East and West, the Mary and the Martha, can never meet to make perfect the realization of truth. And in spite of our material poverty and the antagonism of time I wait patiently for this meeting.

Robinson Crusoe's island comes to my mind when I think of an institution where the first great lesson in the perfect union of man and nature, not only through love but through active communication, may be learnt unobstructed. We have to keep in mind the fact that love and action are the only media through which perfect knowledge can be obtained, for the object of knowledge is not pedantry but wisdom. An institution of this kind should not only train up one's limbs and mind to be ready for all emergencies, but to be attuned to the response between life and the world, to find the balance of their harmony which is wisdom. The first important lesson for children in such a place would be that of improvisation, the ready-made having been banished in order to give constant occasion to explore one's capacity through surprise achievements. I must make it plain that this implies a lesson not in simple life, but in creative life. For life may grow complex, and yet, if there is a living personality at its centre, it will have the unity of creation, it will carry its own weight in perfect grace, and will not be a mere addition to the number of facts that only go to swell a crowd.

I wish I could say that we have fulfilled this dream in our school. We have only made a beginning. We have given the children an opportunity to find their freedom in nature by being able to love it. For love is freedom; it saves us from paying with our soul for objects that are all too cheap. I know men who preach the cult of the simple life by glorifying the spiritual merit of poverty. I refuse to imagine any special value in poverty when it is a mere negation. Only when the mind is sensitive to the deeper call of reality is it weaned away from the lure of the fictitious. It is callousness which robs us of our simple power to enjoy and dooms us to the indignity of snobbish pride in furniture and the foolish burden of expensive things. But to pit the callousness of asceticism against the callousness of luxury is to fight one evil with another, inviting the pitiless demon of the desert in place of the indiscriminate demon of the jungle.

With the help of literature, festive ceremonials and religious teachings I tried to develop in the children of my school their feeling for Nature as also a sensitiveness to their human surroundings. I prepared for them a real home-coming into this world. Among the subjects they learnt in the open air, in the shade of trees, were music and painting, and they had their dramatic performances.

But this was not sufficient, and I waited for men and the means to be able to introduce into our school activities that would build up character. I felt the need of the western genius for imparting to my educational ideal the strength of reality which knew how to achieve a definite end of practical good.

The obstacles were numerous. The tradition of the community which calls itself educated, the parents' expectations, the upbringing of the teachers themselves, the claim and the constitution of the official University, were all overwhelmingly arrayed against the idea I cherished. In addition, we attracted hardly any contributions from my countrymen as our funds were inadequate to support an institution in which the number of boys had necessarily to be small.

Fortunately, help came to us from an English friend who took the leading part in creating and guiding the rural organization connected with Visva-Bharati. He believes, as I do, in an education which takes count of the organic wholeness of human individuality, needing a general stimulation of all faculties, bodily and mental. In order to have the freedom to give effect to this idea, we started our work with a few boys who were orphans or whose parents were too poor to be able to send them to any kind of school.

Before long we discovered that minds actively engaged in constructive work fast developed energies which sought eager outlet in the pursuit of knowledge, even to the extent of undertaking extra tasks. The minds of these boys became so alert that a very simple fact made them at once see the advantage of learning English, which was not in their course of studies. The idea came to them one day when they were posting some letters: on the envelopes the post-master wrote in English the addresses that had already been written in Bengali. Immediately they went to their teacher asking that they be taught English in an additional hour. These boys never regretted their rash request. Yet I remember to this day what criminal thoughts used to fill my young mind when my own teacher of English showed himself at the bend of the lane leading to our house!

For these boys vacation has no meaning. Their studies, though strenuous, are not a task, being permeated by a holiday spirit which takes shape in activities in their kitchen, their vegetable garden, their weaving, their work of small repairs. It is because their classwork has not been separated from their normal activities but forms a part of their daily current of life, that it easily carries itself by its own onward flow.

Most of our boys when they first came were weak in body and mind; the ravages of malaria and other tropical diseases had been their fatal inheritance. They brought with them an intolerable mental perversity; the Brahmin was supercilious, the non-Brahmin pitiable in his shrinking self-abasement. They hated to do any work of common good lest others besides themselves should get the least. They sulked when they were asked to do for their own benefit the kind of work that, they thought, should be done by a paid servant. They were not averse to living on charity but were ashamed of self-help.

It might have been thought that this meanness and moral lethargy were inherent in their nature. But within a very short time all that changed. The spirit of sacrifice and comradeship which these boys have developed is rare even in children who have had better opportunities. It was the active, healthy life which brought out all that was good in them and the accumulated rubbish of impurities was swept off. The daily work which they were doing gave rise to problems which demanded a solution. The logic of facts showed to them the reality of moral principles in life, and now they feel astonished when other boys do not understand such principles. They take great pleasure in cooking, weaving, gardening, improving their surroundings, and in rendering services to other boys, very often secretly, lest they should feel embarrassed. The members of a mess usually clamour for more than is provided for them, but these boys willingly simplify their needs. They have developed a sense of responsibility. Instead of grumbling at deficiencies, they think and manage for themselves. To improve their dietary they must apply extra zest on their vegetable patches. Even if they get poor results, these have a value not to be assessed in terms of market price.

To give an artistic touch to my description, I wish I could speak of some break-down in our plan, of some unexpected element of misfit trying to wreck the symmetry of our arrangements. I have to confess, however, that it has not yet happened. Perhaps our tropical climate is accountable for this dull calm in our atmosphere, for the lack of that excess energy which often loves to upset things. Maybe it is not too late to hope that this experiment of ours is not going to be a model paradise for harmless boys. Some incalculable problems, I am sure, will presently arise, challenging our theories and our faith in our ideal.

Meanwhile, having realized that this daily practice in the adaptation of mind and body to life's necessities has made these boys intellectually alert, we have mustered courage to extend the system to the primary section of our school. The children of that section, under an ideal teacher who believes that to teach is to learn, have just finished constructing their first hut of which they are absurdly proud. They have apparently begun to think that education is a permanent part of the adventure of life; it is not like a painful hospital treatment for curing them of the congenital malady of their ignorance, but is a function of health, the natural expression of their mind's vitality. Thus, I have just had the good fortune to watch the first shoot of life peeping out in a humble corner of our organization. My idea is to allow this creeper to grow, with no special label of learned nomenclature attached to it; grow till it completely hides the dead pole that bears no natural flower or fruit, but flourishes the parchment flag of examination success.

Before I stop I must say a few more words about a most important item on our educational programme.

Children have their active sub-conscious mind which, like the tree, has the power to draw food from the surrounding atmosphere. For them the atmosphere is a great deal more important than rules and methods, equipment, textbooks and lessons. The earth has her mass of substance in her land and water; but, if I may use figurative language, she finds her stimulus in her atmosphere. It evokes from her responses in colour and perfume, music and movement. In his society man has about himself a diffuse atmosphere of culture. It keeps his mind sensitive to his racial inheritance, to the current of influences that come from tradition; it enables him to imbibe unconsciously the concentrated wisdom of ages. But in our educational organizations we behave like miners, digging only for things and not like the tillers of the earth whose work is a perfect collaboration with nature.

I tried to create an atmosphere in my school—this was the main task. In educational institutions our faculties have to be nourished in order to give our mind its freedom, to make our imagination fit for the world which belongs to art, and to stir our sympathy for human relationships. This last is even more important than learning the geography of foreign lands.

The minds of the children of today are almost deliberately made incapable of understanding other people with different languages and customs. The result is that, later, they hurt one another out of ignorance and suffer from the worst form of the blindness of the age. The Christian missionaries themselves help in this cultivation of contempt for alien races and civilizations. Led by sectarian pride while they profess brotherhood for all, they use school textbooks to corrupt young susceptible minds. I have tried to save our children from such aberrations, and here the help of friends from the West, with their sympathetic hearts, has been of the greatest service.

—1926

Children run out of the temple
and play in the dust.
God watches their games
and forgets the priest.

Rabindranath Tagore

4

ON THE EVE OF DEPARTURE

Our hermitage stands in the midst of fields. Here, in the heart of nature, live the old and the young, the teacher and the taught, sharing a common life. The morning sun touches us with its first beams, and the stars of the night shine upon our upturned faces. When the storm rises, we see its dusty warning a-swing in the far horizon. The first news of the season's change appears in the leaves of the trees that surround us. We do not shut out nature from our lives; it comes to us directly and with ease.

Yet we like to have here in-our isolation an equally direct touch with the world outside. We wish to see the storms that hit mankind, the many changes, the sunrises and sunsets, that occur in the story of man. Away as we are from the busy centres of life, we have the advantage of accepting the world's happenings as they are, and not recast in this mould of thinking or that; we can view them all in the right perspective.

In order to relate the life of our little country school with the world at large, we feel the need to travel around the world. And the world invites us. It is not possible, though, for all two hundred of us to launch out in response to this invitation. So I am accepting it on behalf of you all. Through me, all of you will reap the benefits of this travel. I shall store up something of the outside world within myself and bring it back for you when I return to your hermitage.

We will talk a lot about it then. Meanwhile, let me clear up one or two matters on the eve of departure.

Many have asked me, "Why do you want to travel in Europe?" and I have not known how to answer them. If I said it was to be travel for travel's sake, they would think I was begging the question. It is hard to set minds at ease unless the full inventory of an action with the profit and loss involved was given.

It is only in our country that people ask why a man should go somewhere without reason. The natural desire to travel is something that we cannot understand. We are so strongly tied to our homes, and the very thought of moving out is so much inhibited by fear of the inauspicious and tears of parting, that the world has slipped away from our purview. Our kinfolk make such a close circle that all who are beyond it appear unrelated. That is why, inevitably, we have to answer many questions when we want to step out even for a brief while. For wings stiffened by disuse, the joy in sheer flying is beyond comprehension.

When I first went abroad, I was young, and the material purpose of trying to qualify for the Civil Service or the Bar made a plausible excuse for travel. Today, at the age of fifty-two, I cannot advance any such reason and must look for an excuse of a spiritual kind.

People in India admit the need for travel for a spiritual purpose. Those who are ready to ascribe that purpose to me yet wonder what good it would do if I went abroad. After all, salvation lies in visiting holy places and people—in India.

I say that my purpose is simply to go. I am lucky to have been born on this earth and it will be real satisfaction to see as much of it as I can. I have been blessed with a pair of eyes and their fulfilment lies in beholding the vastness of the world in as many aspects as possible.

Yet I admit that I also look forward to profit. I want not only to feel the pleasures of travel, but to attain through them some kind of objective.

A European who travels in India with respect in his heart reaps, I believe, the benefits of a pilgrimage. I have known such Europeans and have great regard for them. Not that the glory of India has to be revealed to me through the foreigners' appreciation! I bow before the strength of their spirit—the power to penetrate the guise of the unfamiliar and discover any good behind it is rare. The power to move freely in the realm of truth is not tested until one visits other lands. The petty-souled accept the familiar as the only truth and reject all else as un-important or unreal. The test of our devotion to truth lies in the ability to push open the doors of the unfamiliar, discover what lies behind and pay homage, homage that is not dictated by blind custom and is given with a free mind.

A visit to Europe can be the most fruitful pilgrimage for an Indian if his mind is not cluttered with ancient bias and his eyes seek truth. Europeans who have come to India in a spirit of pilgrimage have not failed to see the miseries of our outer aspect of life; yet, through the dust of appearances, they have also seen the realities beyond.

Not that the realities are all bare to the view in Europe either. The difference is that they lie hidden, not under tatters but behind a screen of glamour, which probably makes them even more difficult to perceive. We may well be dazzled by the bejewelled screen and be deluded into thinking that it is the worthiest object the West has to show, and we may come back without even a glimpse of the deity behind the screen.

If we carry with us the presupposition that the bejewelled screen is all that exists, then our journey will be an utter waste.

A cliche that has gained currency is that European civilization is materialistic and soulless. That idea does not have to be supported by facts. What some say, others echo; numbers sanctify, and take the place of reason.

We must first of all remind ourselves that wherever there is some good, there must be spiritual strength behind it. For truth can be achieved only through the spirit, not through machines, no matter how powerful. If we see any progress in Europe, behind it indubitably is the power of the spirit; it cannot be the creation of dead matter. It is the power of the spirit that manifests itself in things material.

To say that Europe does not express the human spirit but merely accumulates material things is as good as saying that a tree does not express its life through the dead leaves which it sheds. It is the force of life in the tree that makes it shed its leaves, the dead leaves are no sign of its own death. Only life can die at every moment—true death comes when death ceases.

Man in modern Europe is engaged in constant experimentation and change. What he accepts today, he discards tomorrow. He refuses to stand still. There are many who see in this changefulness a lack of profundity.

Everything in the universe is enclosed in a cycle of death and rebirth. Yet, have not our sages said of the same universe that all is born out of joy? It is through death that the immortal expresses itself ceaselessly. When we mistake the outward for the ultimate, we can neither perceive the soul nor feel happy about accepting the outward. Europe too has a soul and it does not lack in strength. When we discover Europe's spiritual core, we also discover its inner reality—something that is neither materialistic nor simply of the intellect, but is sheer joy of life.

What I am trying to say may be illustrated by a recent incident. A ship with two thousand passengers, crossing the Atlantic, struck a floating iceberg at dead of night. When it was about to sink, the men aboard—European and American—struggled to save the lives of the women and children instead of their own. This terrible accident suddenly drew the curtain aside, as it were, and gave us a glimpse of the inner selves of these men, so that we bowed our heads in admiration and exultant response.

Not long since, some friends of ours were returning from Dacca along the river by steam launch. At midstream a boat was accidentally hit by the launch, overturned, and its three occupants were about to drown. Everyone on the launch called out to another boat passing by, but it sailed away without a second look. There was no danger, no difficulty, in rescuing the lives; yet those boatmen did not care.

This reminds me of another incident. A storm had raged all night; the wind had fallen at break of day but the river was still turbulent. My boat was anchored off shore. Suddenly I thought I saw a woman's body floating down the river, only her long tresses of hair visible above the water. I called out to people near about, urging them to take my life-boat and hasten to the rescue in case the woman was still alive. No one moved. Then I offered to give five rupees to everyone who would go. Immediately a number of men rushed out with a boat and brought back the unconscious woman who recovered after a while. Had it not been for the reward, her life would have been lost.

On another occasion, I was crossing a vast shallow stretch of water by boat. Where the lake meets the river, fishermen often put up posts to narrow down the passage of the water. That helps them to catch fish but makes the current fast and fearful, and I have seen many a boat in distress at such points. Passing through a narrow outlet between posts, my boat got stuck at a dangerous spot. Within a few yards there were fishermen at work but they did not heed our appeal for help. Our boatmen now announced a reward but the fishermen played deaf to raise the bid, even though our trouble was due entirely to their action. When the offer grew to a tidy sum, the men suddenly regained their hearing!

You will recall that when a shop was on fire in Bolpur Bazar some time back, it was four Afghans who helped you to put it out, not the people of the neighbourhood. They in fact refused to let you have their water pitchers which would become contaminated by the touch of Afghan hands.

There is no need to pile instances of this poverty of spirit that we see all the time. Whatever we might say in self-defence, at heart we cannot help admitting this lack of character.

Is selflessness totally unrelated to spirituality? Is spirituality attained only by withdrawal from the world and chanting the Holy Name in the sanctity of isolation? Is it not soul force that truly makes men brave?

In the incident of the sinking of the *Titanic,* we suddenly saw a group of men confronted by death and yet bathed in a shining light. This incident did not throw up the exceptional calibre of any one individual. What, indeed, was most remarkable was the willing self-sacrifice of rich men brought up in luxury and vaunting class superiority. They all stood aside of their own accord, making way for the weak and the infirm.

Sudden disaster tends to release the primitive instincts in man, stripped of the discipline of civilization. When there is time to think, there is a chance for self-control. On that dark night on the *Titanic,* as people were either fast asleep or in the thick of gaiety, they were rudely awakened to find themselves face to face with the sudden spectre of death. Yet they were not maddened by panic, they did not fight to save their own lives. Not that the heroism thus revealed was fortuitous, or even a personal virtue; it was the dramatization of a national trait acquired by long self-discipline. It was the victory of the human spirit over death.

Is not the same spiritual strength, so intensely revealed in this incident, visible in many forms and aspects in the life of the western world? There are countless instances of the total denial of self for the sake of the country and the community. Out of the cumulative effect of such sacrifices the civilization of Europe has risen—as a coral island rises out of the sea.

No society can achieve true progress except through suffering and for that the materialist has no capacity whatsoever. Why should he discard material things if his only happiness lies in them? People are willing enough to suffer to gain merit, as prescribed in the scriptures, since it is to them as useful as worldly goods. But no worshipper of material objects alone can give his life for the sake of a virtue that is only a free impulse of the heart.

In Europe, every day, we see instances of the eager acceptance of suffering for the sake of the nation, for mankind, for love and for the expansion of knowledge, impelled only by the heart's promptings.

Not all of this is genuine, a good deal is mere bravado. But that does not justify any attempt to belittle what is genuine. On certain nights there appears around the moon a circle of light which we know is an illusion; however, even that illusion has to appear around the moon, which is very real. Reflected glory surrounds true light in every society, but the illusion, far from disproving, only proves the existence of that light.

We have read of the astounding men of the West, we have not seen them at close quarter. The ones we have seen do not rank among Europe's luminaries. A long time ago we met a Swede named Hammergren. He had happened to read about Rammohan Ray, and stirred to deep feeling for India he came over to this country—it was far from easy because of his lack of means. He did not know the people or the language, yet he took up his abode in a Bengali home and made Rammohan Ray's country his own. His days were numbered, but those who knew him will never forget how he served our people with steadfast devotion while he had to bear great hardship. Yet, when his body was cremated at Nimtolla Ghat, one of our weekly journals lamented the "defilement" of a Hindu cremation ground!

All of you know how Sister Nivedita, inspired by her devotion to Swami Vivekananda, dedicated her life to India in supreme consecration.

Both these examples are of people whose self-effacement took place under conditions far removed from the familiar ways of their experience. Everything they faced was totally opposed to their instincts. It was not their sacrifice alone—they even had to carve out their own path of sacrifice, since all known paths were forbidden to them.

Undoubtedly, it was from their national character that they drew this idealism and the srength to give themselves to it. Could such amazing strength come from a materialist tradition? Was it not truly spiritual strength, the like of which is not often to be seen in our country?

Far be it for me to say that there is no spirituality in our country. Here, too, an aspect of it has found clear expression. The true devotee among us has the power to discern either through the eyes of knowledge or through feeling the one ultimate manifested in the fragmented many. Behind this power lies the steady contemplation and striving of many centuries. That is why the holy ones in this land find easy communion with the infinite.

A sensitive foreigner who visits our country in quest of this side of our national character is sure to find what he seeks and it may fill a certain void in him. But there is a like void within us which needs to be filled—it has been the cause, since long, of much of our weakness and fatigue.

The proud traditionalist will retort that what we lack is not spirituality; we lack that knowledge of material things which has enabled the West to dominate over the world.

But then, no nation has ever achieved progress simply through material things or gained power merely by worldly wisdom. It is not enough to pour oil into the lamp and prepare a wick skilfully—you have to light the lamp somehow.

A cynic alone may say that Europe rules all the world by its material power. The true source of its strength is spiritual. In no other way can that strength be accounted for.

Everyone will admit that Buddhism is not a religion of material gains. Yet during its rise and the period of its dominance, science, industry and imperial power rose to heights which were never again attained in our history. The reason is that, when the human spirit is released from stagnation, its power expands and seeks to grow in every direction. Spirituality is intrinsic to all strength, fulfilment is in its very nature. It does not ever seek to defeat itself by restraining man's development, within or without.

Whatever may be the outward aspect of Europe's power, I have no doubt that at its core is the power of the spirit.

And this is a conscious power. It cannot ignore any human suffering, any denial. It is forever harnessed to the strenuous effort to remove miseries of all kinds. What except the immortal spirit can give strength to the active goodwill behind this effort, the goodwill that drags man out of his cosy bed and impels him into acts of self-sacrifice and makes him listen even to the call of death?

A spiritual seed from the tree of Christ's life entered the soil of Europe's consciousness and led to rich fruit-bearing. What is the living force within that seed? It is the ability to find strength in suffering.

For hundreds of years Europe has heard, in songs and prayers and rituals, the message of the Heavenly mercy which makes all human suffering its own. Through the ages this idea has entered the core of the European mind, occupying the secret depths of the subconscious, where the seed is cast and the basis laid of all human endeavour.

That is why we constantly see in Europe instances of people who profess against Christianity and sing the praises of materialism and yet sacrifice themselves so unreservedly when the need arises, bearing all sorrow and ridicule with heroism. Without even being aware of it, they place the immortal values above the mortal and the welfare of all above personal satisfactions.

Those on the *Titanic* who scorned their own peril to save the lives of others were not all devout Christians. There were perhaps many among them who professed atheism and agnosticism. But how could they dissociate themselves from their spiritual tradition by merely professing a different creed? He who has given his life to a cause is striving single-handed for the people as a whole. The multitude of people in their stupidity may sneer at him, and yet they will be beneficiaries in the fruits of his achievement.

However unpleasant it may be, we must admit that neither the capacity nor the effort to bear the sorrows of others, intrinsic in the love of God, is widely evident in our country. The emotional aspect of devotion in all its intensity, the nuances of feelings, the various fervours, are to be found in us in abundance; not so, the urge for service and self-sacrifice, the strength to bear sufferings with ease. We have sought the delights of divine love to the exclusion of its pains.

There is no spirituality in the cultivation of suffering for some ultimate gain; true spirituality lies in suffering for the sake of love. The agonies of the man always in search of wealth or the penances of the man in search of a secure place in the next world, cannot lead to fulfilment; they only denote an inner poverty. The sacrifice that stems out of love alone elevates the spirit to great heights of strength and joy and helps life to triumph over death.

It is the joy in suffering that makes us transcend our own selves and apprehend the universal. Suffering is the price of truth. It is an enrichment of the spirit. Through suffering the spirit expresses its strength, and through it we understand ourselves, and humanity. So it is that the scriptures tell us: "The spirit is not attainable by the strengthless." In other words, he who does not have the strength to suffer cannot attain self-realization.

We have failed to draw close to one another through suffering. How can we call our people our own without paying the price for it? Even a mother has to pay her price in suffering and in service to make her child her own. We pay this price, unbidden, for whatever we accept as true values. But then, we have failed to accept the people around us in our hearts and cannot, therefore, find any joy in an act of sacrifice on their account.

It is only through the inner vision, which is love, that we apprehend the reality of others. When philosophy tells us that all beings arc one, it is only an abstraction which helps us little in equating all with one's self. That is achieved only through love, which is the power of the spirit, endless in patience, joyous in self-dedication. It is by virtue of this power that the patriot realizes the universal spirit in his country, and the humanist realizes it in all mankind.

Europe's religion is the religion of love, of suffering that expresses itself in service, and it brings man closer to man. The undying flame of suffering is its sacrificial fire, kept alive by die thousands of devotees who give themselves to it, imparting energy to the entire nation. From this intense sacrifice is born that force of immortality which expresses itself in science and the arts, literature, politics and commerce. Those cannot be machine-made, but have to be created through penance, and the fire of penance is the fire of the spirit, the power of the religion of man.

So it is that, in the Buddhist period when India accepted the religion of love and self-denial, she attained a development akin to Europe's today. Medical care was available not only to the human being, but to lower animals as well; the effort to alleviate the sufferings of all living creatures appeared in a variety of ways. Religious leaders crossed impassable barriers to go to foreign lands and redeem benighted aliens, at the cost of great hardship to themselves. India, at that time, gave her devotees strength and nobility through suffering, and so she was able to conquer not only her soul but the world. She brought together spiritual and material progress at a time when Europe's Christian civilization was not even a dream. The glow of that penance and self-denial has now been dimmed by artificiality and emotionalism, but has it been lost altogether? If we see it in others, shall we not be reminded of what is within ourselves?

We must remember that where the fire blazes brightly, ashes must also be there in plenty. A tiny flame gives little heat; its effects are scanty and its destructive aspect is timid.

It must be admitted that sin appears in Europe in terrifying proportions, as a raging restlessness, the like of which we do not see in our country. Yet the people of Europe are not resigned to that state; it has made them all the more vigilant. They boldly challenge every form of demon, from the malarial mosquito to the social maladies, even if they have to stake life itself in the conflict. "A little virtue" says the *Geeta,* "saves us from a mighty fear." That particle of virtue in a society out-weighs the most colossal corruption.

There is deviation from justice in Europe's treatment of weaker peoples; but that deviation is not the only reality. From within its very greed, cruel and power-drunk as it is, arises the voice crying shame on itself. There is no dearth in Europe of heroic souls who stand firmly against the tyranny of the mighty. Such upright men do not hesitate to take sides with alien peoples in far-off lands and suffer on their account. Who indeed are the true friends of the Indians seeking self-government for their country? Heedless of resistance and scorn, they urge their own countrymen to give up self-interest for the sake of justice. They are apparently few in number, but not truly so. For these men are more than themselves; they are part of a tradition. They do not all work at the same time or towards the same ends; but they are the true conscience of society. They are the knights who have undertaken to defend the weak. They tread in the hard path of Christ, stained with the blood of the divine leader who took the sorrows of the world upon himself to save the soul of man and to lead him from darkness into light. Deep within the heart of Europe that light still shines.

We, on the other hand, constantly seek consolation in telling ourselves that we are a spiritual, God-fearing people, and have little thought for mundane things—hence our lack of progress in worldly affairs. That is how we try to reduce our shame of poverty; there are many among us who even proudly declare poverty to be our main asset.

But poverty is glorious only in those who are capable of being rich. There is glory in the sacrifice of wealth but none in forced poverty. Poverty brings no honour to people who are half-dead from lack of food; who seek somehow to survive; who, because they are poor, exploit the poor at the first opportunity, and because they are powerless, strike at the weak as soon as they have power.

Our poverty and humiliation was not the result of virtue which expands the spirit. We have confined spirituality to the private cult of devotion instead of summoning all humanity to it. Our religious bigotry has made us unfit for anything but slavery. Our woes, we fondly imagine, can be ended by legislation and we can become full-fledged human beings when we obtain seats in the legislature. But a nation's progress is not achieved mechanically. It cannot be achieved until we are prepared to pay the price.

So it is that, if the journey to Europe is undertaken in the spirit of a pilgrimage, it cannot be in vain. We have our guru there too—in the innermost force of Europe's people. The guru has to be sought for, everywhere, with eyes of reverence—it is not enough just to look around. In our blindness and pride we may come back without having seen him, and with the idea that England's might lies in her Parliament and Europe's richness is factory-made, that all the greatness of the West is a matter of armaments and commerce and other material objects.

People who have no true awareness of strength within themselves are apt to assume that strength lies in outward things, and once those are gained everything will be won. But Europe asks, echoing the voice of ancient India, "What shall I do with that which will not make me immortal?" She knows that greatness is not the product of railways, telegraph poles, factories and techniques. That is why Europe has taken the hero's vow of truth, dedicating to it her wealth and her life, and with every mistake, every failure, renewing her enterprise with heightened zeal. Evil appears from time to time like fire from friction, poison from the "churning of the ocean," but she refuses to take evil for granted. Her soldiers are brave and their weapons keen, and their dedication to truth makes them deathless. And we on our part have been too lazy even to face truth, too indifferent to seek it, as we lie wrapped in the self-made bondage which we have mistaken for shelter.

Small wonder, then, that when there is a crisis and there is no way but the way of truth, we cannot accept the challenge of the occasion. We continue to play and call it work, live in illusion and expect the benefits of reality. We fail to keep up our fake enthusiasms to complete the work in hand, and caught in the meshes of theorizing and sentimentality, stumble repeatedly in our tasks. Hence the journey to Europe in the spirit of a pilgrim seeking to realize the highest values of life cannot be vain. But the pilgrim should go forth in a spirit of reverence, and the enrichment of the human personality should be his quest.

There is, I know, a point of conflict between the West and ourselves—self-interest—which hurts us in so many ways. It hurts us despite the fact that it has arisen out of our own spiritual poverty and is an atonement for sins accumulated. Arrogance is the mask with which our opponents conceal their pettiness of mind, and in their blind conceit they deny any good in all but themselves. Bearing as we do this deep wound, it is not easy for us to understand and accept what is good in Europe. We mistrust the religious force behind Europe's civilization and dismiss it as coarsely materialistic. We fear the contamination of the spirit which might lead us to put power on the pedestal of truth and prostrate ourselves before it in humble worship. We fear lest we fail to accept the other's worth in an honourable way and simply give up our own beliefs in weary self-deprecation; lest we indulge in hollow imitation, become the shadow of the other, and thus cease-to exist.

These are the hazards which make this journey a pilgrimage of truth. We have to overcome the obstacles and bear the pains of a difficult approach. We have to cast aside the futile burden of self-importance and yet guard with care the materials of our true pride. Indeed, it is the difficulties that make the journey worth while, for what is easily attained does not become a part of our being. And yet, all true gain must mean a fuller unfolding of consciousness. In other words, whatever we truly achieve must lead to greater self-realization. If it does not, outward gains remain outward, and as illusory as all such things are.

—1912

The rose is a great deal more
than a blushing apology
for its thorn.
Rabindranath Tagore

5

EAST AND WEST

The History of India—of whom is it the Story?

In the remote past the white-skinned Aryans had to overcome the stupendous barriers of nature along with the resistance of man to force their entry into India. As they swept aside the enveloping curtain of thick dark forests, a bright and far-stretching land rich with the varied produce of its soil was revealed. With intelligence, strength and united effort the Aryans laid the foundations of India's history. But they never proclaimed, "This is our India."

They began to merge with the indigenous non-Aryans. Even in the first flush of their racial predominance they took non-Aryan women in marriage. This intermixture became more and more free in the Buddhist age. Towards the end of that period, Brahminic society began to react against the marital freedom, and to refix racial boundaries, making them impregnable. But things had already gone so far that in many parts of the country it was difficult to get a Brahmin of pure blood even for religious rites. Brahmins had often to be brought from distant places or new groups of them had to be created, under royal command, by investiture with the sacred thread. The white skin on which the Aryans prided themselves had meanwhile darkened, and Sudra ritual and tradition had been absorbed in their social polity. The larger "Hindu" society, evolving thus, was not only apart from the Aryan community of the Vedic times, but was in many respects even antagonistic.

The history of India, however, did not come to an end there. Providence would not let her say that her history belonged to the Hindu alone. While the Rajput kings were engaged in fighting one another with great heroism in a suicidal civil war, the Muslims from beyond India took advantage of this division in the country, swept in through the breaches and spread out in every direction; generation after generation of them lived and died here, and thus they made this land their own.

If we draw a line at this point, crying, "Stop! We need go no further," and regard India's history as the history of the Hindu and the Muslim, will the great Architect who is ever at work enlarging the sphere of human relationships alter his plans simply to suit our vanity?

Whether India is to belong more to the Hindu or to the Muslim, or whether some other race is to achieve a greater supremacy—that is not the problem with which Providence is troubled. It is not as if, in the court of the Almighty, the advocates of different parties are engaged in pleading the rival claims of Hindu, Muslim and Westerner, and the party that wins the decree shall finally plant its banner of victory and permanent possession. It is our vanity which makes us think that there is a battle between contending rights—the only battle is the eternal one for the vindication of truth.

What is good and true is for all, and we see it establish itself in spite of obstacles and contrary forces. But the extent of its progress has to depend on our efforts for its furtherance. There is no place in the universal scheme of things for a man of ambition to rest for ever on the peak of triumph, triumph for himself or for his race. That Alexander failed to bring the world under the banner of Greece only proves the futility of such designs; Greece's arrogant ambition has no meaning for us today. The Roman dream of a world-empire was foiled by the barbarians—and whoever deplores that blow to Rome's imperial pride? Greece and Rome have laden the golden boat of Time with the ripe harvests of their culture; that they themselves failed to get into the boat proved no loss, but rather lightened its load.

The objective of Indian history is not to set up Hindu or some other dominance, but to secure a special kind of fulfilment for humanity, a level of perfection that must be a gain for all. In the course of this fulfilment, if Hindu, Muslim and the British have to submerge the aggressive parts of their individuality, it may be hurtful to their national pride but it will not be reckoned as a loss in the scales of truth and human rights.

We are all here to build up Greater India. We are only one of the many elements required for the purpose; if any one element becomes mutinous and claims an undue predominance, refusing to blend with the others, that will somewhat retard the pace of construction. The part that wishes to remain separate will have to be cast aside; but the component which knows it is nothing by itself and is dedicated to the entire scheme, will lose only its pettiness and find permanence in the mighty whole.

So the part of India which seeks to stay isolated in the sanctuary of a remote past will be crushed and made one with all by the Dispenser of India's destiny; or else, it will be abandoned as a useless impediment. India's history is not the story of the Hindu alone. We are part material in that history; and if we cannot fit ourselves into the scheme, it is we who shall have to go. If we stand aloof in our "purity", passing on this pride of isolation to succeeding generations, if we make our religion and social customs exclusively our own, our places of worship forbidden to outsiders and our ancient lore kept under lock and key, then we shall simply proclaim to the world that we have been condemned to death in the court of humanity; in the cells we have built for ourselves we await the day of the sentence.

In recent times the British have come to occupy an important place in India's history. That is not an accident. Without this contact with the West, India would have remained incomplete. Europe has lighted her lamp; we have to light ours from that flame and set out once more on our journey along the paths of time. We are not so unfortunate, nor is the world so poor, that it has nothing more to give us because, three thousand years ago, our forefathers extracted from it everything it could yield! If it were true that whatever needed to be done had already been done in the past, once and for all, then our continued existence would only be a burden to the earth. How can those who think they had attained their completeness in their ancestors and must insulate their beliefs and practices against the touch of modernism, have the urge to live in the present, or have any faith in the future?

Like messengers from heaven the British have come through the breach in our crumbling walls and entered our homes to inspire in us the faith that the world needs us too—not where we are confined within narrow bounds but in wider fields of knowledge, work, new discoveries. Until we answer their call and march in step with them, they will torment us and rob us of our complacent sleep. For India, continuing the process of growth, is of vital interest to all the world's peoples. Who are we to say that this country is ours alone? In fact, who is this "We"? Bengali, Marathi, or Punjabi, Hindu or Muslim? Only the larger "We" in whom all these—Hindu and Muslim and British and whoever else there be—must eventually unite, shall have the right to determine what is India and what is of the outside.

We who have the task of building up this Greater India must make our contact with the British yield good results. We cannot remain aloof, unresponsive, heedless of any give-and-take—that would mean impoverishment of India's history itself.

So the noblest men of modern India have made it their lifework to bring East and West together. There has been, for instance, Rammohan Ray. He stood alone in his day for

India's union with the world on the broad basis of humanity. No blind belief, no ancestral habit obscured his vision. With a wonderful breadth of heart and intellect he accepted the West without renouncing the East and, single-handed, brought the new Bengal into being. Boldly he faced persecution in his endeavour to gain for us the inalienable rights of man in the pursuit of truth, to make us realize that we also have inherited the earth. It was he who first felt and declared that, for us the Buddha, Christ and Muhammad had lived; that, for each one of us has been stored up the discipline of our ancient sages; that, whoever has removed obstacles from the path of knowledge or released the energies of man from stagnation, is our very own, and through this kinship all of us are vested with glory.

Rammohan Ray built a bridge between India and Europe and remains, to this day, an inspiration in all our creative activities. No prejudice or pride could make him deny the purpose of Time, the purpose that has not spent itself up in the past but moves onward to fulfilment in the future.

In South India Ranade devoted his life to the building of such a bridge. He had the faculty of synthesis which abolishes discord and makes for freedom of will. Constantly engaged in resolving the conflict of ideas and interests, he cleared the path for the acceptance of whatever was of value in the British contribution to our history.

The great-souled Vivekananda, whose death we mourned recently, took a similar stand. He had the genius to accept, harmonize and recreate, and he dedicated himself to the exchange of ideals between India and the West.

There also had been the day when Bankimchandra, in the pages of *Bangadarshan,* invited his readers to a real festival of the union of East and West. That note of universality in Bengali literature has made wonderful progress since, and is in accord with world literary trends.

Many of us who belong to the educated class seem to think that the attempt to unite all racial elements on our soil is meant to serve a political purpose. That is simply to belittle a great endeavour by giving it a petty motive. For us in India, to attain unity is by itself an objective far more worthy than any other. Failing in this aim, we lose a basic principle of life and let all our power become fettered and feeble.

It is from the view-point of the broad religion of man that we must look at these efforts to bring about unity—then only will they succeed. But if that truly religious feeling far beyond petty pride and expediency is to be our main urge, the efforts cannot remain confined to Indians alone—they must reach out to the British.

What are we to make of the current conflict between the British and the Indian? Has it no reality? Is it mere illusion created by a group of conspirators? Does it run counter to the trends of our history, as manifested in the concord no less than the clashes between the peoples of this great land? We must try to grasp the meaning of the present dissensions.

In Indian devotional philosophy, opposition is reckoned as one way of attaining union with the Divine; Ravana, for instance, is said to have gained salvation that way. This simply means that the realization of a truth is all the more complete when one has challenged it at first, finally owning up defeat. A ready acquiescence, without question, is not a full acceptance of truth. That is why all science has to be based on stern scepticism.

We were, at one time, overwhelmed by the splendour of Europe and accepted its gifts without discrimination, like beggars. That was not the way to make any real gain. Whether it is knowledge or a political right, it must be earned; that is, it can be real for us only if we win it by struggle with obstructing forces. If someone places it in our hands, by way of alms, we shall not be able to keep it in our possession. We insult ourselves by accepting a thing like that and it does more harm than good.

Hence our reaction against the culture of Europe and its ideals. A newborn sense of self-respect has been prompting us more and more to withdraw into ourselves.

This revulsion has been necessary for the purposes of the history which, as I have said, time is evolving in this land of India. The things we had been accepting from the West without question, in sheer poverty of spirit, could never become our own, since we failed to assess their value and used them only as objects for show. As we realized this, it was only natural that we should ask for a change.

Rammohan Ray was able to assimilate the ideals of Europe so completely because he was not overwhelmed by them; there was no weakness on his side. Firmly rooted in the culture of his own land, he had a standard by which he could evaluate the things he received from others.

This capacity which was natural to the first great architect of the new India has been steadily developing amongst us through conflicting stresses and strains, actions and reactions, so that we are thrown from one extreme to another. We give way, by turns, to eager acceptance and timid rejection, both equally undue, and so we move blindly forward.

One of the causes of the present tension between the British and the Indian is to be found in this strong reaction in sentiment. The continued passive acquiescence in the superior knowledge and strength of the British was making our very souls sick. That sickness was growing by imperceptible degrees, until today it has come to a stage when the spirit of the country is in the grip of a violent revulsion.

There are other causes also. The West has come into our homes and we cannot turn it out like an unwelcome guest. Lacking brotherliness, we defeat the purpose of Time. The West, on the other hand, withholds from us the best it can give, with the same consequences.

If we do not come in contact with what is best in the Englishman, seeing in him only a soldier or merchant or bureaucrat; if he will not stand on the plane where man may commune with man; if, in short, the Indian and the Englishman must stay apart—they will simply be objects of mutual repugnance. Under such conditions the party in power will enact a law of sedition to hold the other's discontent in iron chains, but will succeed only in restraining disaffection without removing it.

There was a time when great-souled Englishmen like David Hare came very near to us and made us feel the nobility of the British character, so that the students of the time freely surrendered their hearts to the foreigner. Today the alien teacher in our schools and colleges does not bring to his students the best that is in his race, but simply lowers the English ideal. Failing to enter into the spirit of English literature as they used to do, they swallow but do not enjoy what is placed before them—the earlier love for Shakespeare and Byron is gone, The understanding which could have come from genuine appreciation of the same literature has thus received a set-back.

Professor or magistrate or merchant or police-chief—take any of these Englishmen in India—and you will see that not one is capable of representing English culture at its best. While denying us the real benefits of the British impact on India, they retard the development of our own capacities and hurt our self-respect. Good laws and efficient administration do not meet all human needs. What is lacking is the human touch. To ask for the human touch and to get mere justice instead, is like asking for bread and receiving a stone. The stone may be rare and precious, but it does not appease hunger.

All the present troubles spring from this failure of East and West to come together. To be near each other and yet never to meet is intolerable and hurtful, and sooner or later the desire to revolt against such a state of things becomes irresistible. This revolt of the spirit is heedless of consequence and prepared even to go to the length of self-destruction.

And yet it is also true that such revulsions are no more than a temporary phase. In spite of all retarding factors our contact with the West must bring about a complete union. There is no escape for us until we have taken from the West whatever is worth while. The unripe fruit must remain joined to its stem—or else it will not ripen at all.

Before I conclude I must say one more word. If the British are not giving us of their best, we are partly to blame. If we shake off our pauperism, then only will they discard their niggardliness. As the Bible says, "Unto everyone that hath shall be given." We must be strong in every way; then only will the British give us what they have come here to give. So long as they look down on us, they cannot fraternize with us. If we stand at their doors with palms outstretched, we shall only be turned away, again and again.

We must awaken their humanity by our own—that is the only way. They themselves have attained what is great and good in them through suffering and toil, and to win such virtues we too have to be strong. To go to the British with bowed heads and folded hands is to arouse what is petty and mean in their character. And to lash out at them in anger is to arouse their evil propensities. If, then, it is true that India has been exciting the insolence, cowardice and inhumanity of the British, it will not do to blame them alone; rather should we take the blame on ourselves.

In their own country social forces are constantly at work subduing the lower nature of the people and encouraging whatever is noble. Social conscience urges each individual to take his stand on a high level and maintain his place there. But the Englishman in India does not belong to society as a whole; he is a member of the Civil Service or the mercantile community or the armed forces, and each of these categories is self-limited, with its own carefully guarded traditions and codes of conduct. So he develops into a strict administrator, or a good businessman, or an out-and-out soldier, and the man in him is lost.

On the other hand, the decadence of the India with which the Englishman gets acquainted cannot possibly evoke the best in him, so that we are both losers. We do not meet the real Englishman but his distorted image—and to this we owe our insults and sufferings.

Sacrifice and service, not hard words and violent action, are true tests of strength. When we have made India our own by applying all our powers for the good of the country, the British in India will have to come to terms with us. So long as we are prompted by individual or social folly to act inhumanly towards our own countrymen, so long as our landlords regard their tenants as their personal property, so long as the strong continue to trample on the weak as part of their ancient privilege, and the higher castes look upon the casteless as worse than beasts—we shall fail to draw out the better qualities in the British and shall ourselves remain ignored and humiliated.

At every turn—in her laws and customs, in her religious and social institutions—India today deceives and insults herself. That is why the meeting of East and West on our soil fails to attain fulfilment. The contact yields nothing but pain. Even if we succeed in pushing out the British by one means or another, this pain will be there; it cannot go until an inner harmony between the two is achieved. Then alone will East and West unite in India; country with country, race with race, knowledge with knowledge, endeavour with endeavour. Then alone will the present chapter of India's history come to its end and a new one start—one of the noblest in the story of Man.

—1908

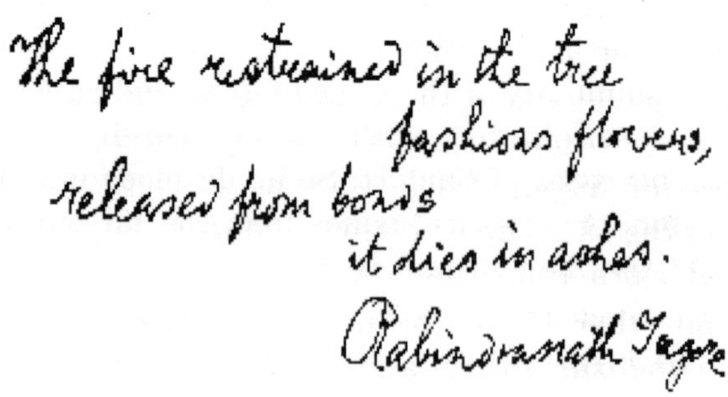

6

THE MASTER'S WILL BE DONE

The wind had only to bring in the rain for our lane to get waterlogged as far as the public thoroughfare. Pedestrians' shoes have then to be carried over their heads like umbrellas, and the inhabitants of the lane appear no fitter than amphibious creatures for the struggle for existence. I have watched this from our verandah year after year ever since my childhood until my hair turned grey.

Meanwhile some sixty years have passed. Steam was then the principal means of transport of our machine age, but electricity has since begun to wink at it mockingly. The atomic theory had then arrived at invisibility, now it has attained incomprehensibility.

Man has now spread his wings in the sky like ants taking wings before death, and the attorneys are counting the days for disputes to arise among claimants for their shares in the sky. The Chinese cut off overnight the pigtails they had worn from time out of mind, and the Japanese took so tremendous a leap over the sea of time as to traverse five hundred years in fifty. But the hospitality of our lane to the rainwater continues unchanged. Even before the foundation stone of the Indian National Congress had been laid, the women of our lane used to sing in the rainy season:

How long will it be, O traveller on foot,
Before you swim across the sea of sorrow?

And today, when Home Rule is within our grasp, and dangling like a ripe fruit just above our moustaches, even today they are singing the same song, in the same tune and rhythm appropriate to the rains.

Always from our childhood we had seen our lane being flooded with rainwater. That is why it never surprised us. One does not worry about matters that are not unexpected. So it was that we did not worry, but acquiesced.

An unmarked word in a letter may fail to catch the eye, but a word that has been underlined is sure to attract attention. This is what happened when not only my mind, but the wheels of my carriage had repeated jolts from the tram-lines that were being laid in pairs in Chitpur Road at the bottom of our lane: the Tramways Company underlined, so to speak, the matter of our lane getting water-logged. Even though the repairs to the tram-lines began with the rainy season, and everything that has a beginning must also have an end according to the science of logic, there is no provision for the repairs ever to end in the science of no-logic followed by the Tramways Company. So it came about that I got soaked in both body and mind while watching the tram-lines being laid, and the stream of men fighting the stream of water. And it was then that I began deeply to ponder: why do we submit?

You have only to set foot in the Chowringhee in the European quarter to realize that you do very well for yourself if you do not endure. We all live in the same town, under the same municipality, but with this difference: the Indians acquiesce, while the Europeans do not. If, after digging up the Chowringhee, and occupying seven-eighths of its width, the Tramways Company had carried on the repairs at the easeful, elephantine pace it had set in Chitpur Road, it would then have had no food by day and no sleep by night.

The meek good men among us will say, "Do you mean

that the tram-lines should be left unrepaired because of some slight inconvenience we must bear otherwise?"

"Of course they should be repaired. But not at a pace so surprisingly comfortable and slow."

"Is that possible?"

The good men among us lack the assurance that things can be better than they are. That is why our streets and lanes are flooded with rainwater. That is why we smear ourselves all over with misery, and spill it like tar out of a cracked barrel.

What I have been saying is not as trivial as it may sound. We have never fully realized that we have any authority over anything. I read in a book about a fish that was kept in a glass jar—how, after hitting its head many times against the jar, it understood at last that glass is not water. Then it was let loose in a large reservoir, where it never acquired the courage to realize that water is not glass; with the result that it kept on going round and round within a small space. Like that fish we too have the fear of hurting our head ingrained in our bones, and we lack the courage to swim freely even where it is safe to do so. Abhimanyu, so our mythology goes, learnt the art of penetrating into the enemy's citadel while his mother was still carrying him in her womb. But he did not learn the art of return, with the result that he was hit in every limb of his body by the seven warriors mounted on chariots. We also learn, before we are born, the art of getting encircled, but not the art of breaking free; and we continue, from the moment we are born, to get involved in everything we think or do; in consequence, we get kicks and blows from everyone, great or small. For generations we have been so used to render implicit obedience to people, books, and even to restrictive gestures and signs, that we fail to realize that we have any authority anywhere in the world.

The greatest thing for man is to know that the possession of authority is the possession of manhood. A country where this knowledge is suppressed under a mass of religious incantations, verses and ritual; where man ties himself up hand and foot in matters of conduct, in order to avoid the slightest aberrations of principle; and where he destroys with his own hands his own roads for fear that they will take him far; such a country teaches boundless disrespect for humanity in the name of spirituality, and opens the largest factory in the world for producing slaves.

Our rulers tell us with scriptural solemnity, "You are incompetent. You will make mistakes. That is why you cannot be entrusted with power."

Those words would have befitted our ancient sages and lawgivers, Manu and Parasar, but they do not sound right in the English voice. So we answer our rulers in the plain language they themselves use when they are not flying high. We say, "To make mistakes is not as big a calamity as not to have authority. Only the freedom to make mistakes confers the freedom to attain truth. We would rather make mistakes than grow lifeless in the expectation of becoming faultless."

We could say more. We could remind our rulers that although they are today riding the motor–car of self-government, they began their political journey in a dogcart at an hour when the twilight before dawn still lingered. On that day the groans of their cartwheels as they slipped into potholes did not exactly sound like a chant of victory. The English Parliament did not travel, right from its beginning, on a paved road that had been smoothed by steam-rollers; throughout its history it has been violently jogged to right and left and has zigzagged from precedent to precedent. It has staggered and lurched through much corruption and conflict, much faction, injustice and mismanagement; and it has served the interest now of the King, now of the Church, now of the landowner, and now of even the brewer. There was a time when members attended Parliament only through fear of censure and fine. Talking of mistakes, we can produce a long list of those made by the British, beginning with Ireland and America in the past and ending with the Boer War, the Dardenelles and Mesopotamia in the present. The list of mistakes they have made in India is not particularly short, but we had better not talk about it. The atrocities committed by the worshippers of Mammon in American politics are not negligible, and the corruption among the French army chiefs exposed by the Dreyfus Affair shows how French politics of the day was dominated by the blind power of the lowest instincts. In spite of all this, no one has the slightest doubt today that only the ever-active impetus of self-government enables man to overcome mistakes through trial, and to struggle and rise to the top after every fall. This is why it is better to let him starve in the effort freely to earn his bread than to offer him the choicest food after he has been enchained.

More significant still, political freedom not only confers the power of good management and the sense of responsibility, it also enlarges the dimensions of the mind. When people who have been circumscribed within village societies and petty social classifications attain political power, they begin to see life in a larger circumference. For lack of this opportunity they have to remain small as men; they cannot see their lives spread over the wide expanse of humanity; and their physical and mental powers, their hopes and expectations, all shrink in consequence. This stunting of a man's soul is a much greater calamity than the loss of his life. *Bhumaiba sukham nalpe sukhamasti*—abundance, not scantiness, gives happiness. We answer our rulers that we accept every possible risk of making mistakes in our demand for self-government; that we are ready to march on, even though we are likely to have occasional falls; and we ask them not to prevent us from marching by harping on the falls.

That is the right answer. An obstinate person who prods the authorities with this answer will be punished by them; on the other hand, he will be acclaimed by the nationalists. Let us now see what will happen if we lay a similar answer before our social leaders. Supposing we tell the rulers of our society that we admit all they say about ourselves: namely, that we live in a depraved age; that we make mistakes when we exercise our freedom of judgment and give offence when we behave freely; that we should disregard our intelligence and accept with bowed heads the precepts taught by sacred books. If we tell the rulers of our society that we admit all this, and yet refuse to insult ourselves by obeying them, their eyes will turn red in anger and they will forthwith pass orders for our social ostracism. People who flap their wings to soar into the political sky keep their feet firmly planted on the social perch.

The heart of the matter is that there is only one rudder for steering a boat to both right and left, one essential principle the mastery of which enables man to be true in both the political and social spheres. The difference between Chitpur Road and the Chowringhee lies in the difference between their attitudes to this principle. Chitpur Road has decided outright that everything is in the hands of the higher authorities, and is therefore lying on its back, doing nothing. The Chowringhee takes the view that it has a right to put its hands to anything that in any way concerns it. It believes that there is the strongest link between itself and the authorities, and by virtue of that belief it has the world in its power. Precisely for lack of that belief Chitpur Road has let the world slip out of its grasp, and rolling up its eyes, is lying comatose.

We have to shut our eyes to think that our narrow homespun rules are the best. On opening our eyes we see a great, principle running through the world. To absorb that principle is to achieve power, prosperity, and happiness. The success of the individual is due to a universal, and not an individual, dispensation. Sure knowledge of this has given the civilization of Europe such a firm basis of power.

But we, in this part of the world, throw up our hands, cast heavy sighs, and say, "The Master's will be done." We give the Master a thousand names, such as father, elder brother, police inspector, priest, pundit, Sitala (goddess of small pox), Manasa (goddess of snakes), Olabibi (goddess of cholera), Dakshin Ray (tiger-god), and the heavenly bodies, Sani, Mangal, Rahu and Ketu. We smash our own power into a thousand bits and cast them to the winds.

The collegians will say, "But we don't invariably observe the old customs and faiths. We are inoculated against small pox, and we are given saline injections when attacked by cholera. Far from regarding the mosquito-borne malaria as a goddess, we regard it as the germ of a germ. Nevertheless, we keep a charmed amulet hanging on our abdomen as a cure for the enlarged spleen which fills it."

Whether we openly admit it or not is immaterial, but the fact remains that our minds are eaten up with the poison of obedience. This cowardice of the mind derives from an undefined, all-embracing fear. Because we do not recognize the universal power that reveals itself as the universal law, we dismiss our intelligence in advance, and give in to a thousand apprehensions. Fear always prompts us to doubt our intelligence, always tells us not to act. I have also seen our rulers forget their western principles as soon as fear creeps in through some chink in their political administration. Then they also blindly break the inviolate law which is the sure foundation of their power. Then they lose faith in the preservation of justice, and consider it more important to preserve their prestige. This indeed is lack of faith in universal dispensation, it is reliance on one's own particular prerogative; and it stems from petty fear, petty greed, or petty subterfuge for simplifying one's task. Driven by blind fear we too are ready to sacrifice our essential manhood, and over-anxious to obey with folded hands everything that exists or does not exist on earth. Whether we study the organic and inorganic sciences, or pass examinations in the history of politics, we cannot cast out of our minds the mystical *mantra*: The Master's Will be Done.

Luckily for the present age, the foundations have been laid in our country of many works of common enterprise. But there is a persistent pressure, thanks to our past, for the common purpose to be transformed into individual interest. From nowhere, and for no purpose whatsoever, a Master pushes his head up. For the sole reason that the individuals who form the group get up, sit down, eat, marry, die, and after death receive oblations from their descendants, at the Master's will. All their problems regarding deeds that are sinful and deeds that are virtuous; regarding the measurement, in cubits, of the perimeter of a well for its water to be suitable for their bath; and the comparative merits, from the same point of view, of wine manufactured by a foreigner and water touched by a heathen;—all their problems they have got permanently solved by assigning them to the Master's will. If we tell them that the water served by a Hindu water-carrier is not fit for drinking because he takes it out of his pail with a dirty mug, but the filtered water served by a Muslim water-carrier is pure and healthy, we hear the answer that it is the language of pettifogging reason and not the Master's will. If we rejoin that it does not matter, that it is not the Master's will, then we shall never again be invited to their homes, and all social intercourse between us will come to an end. These people restrict, at every step and with the most cruel compulsions, their own elementary rights regarding what they will eat or whom they will touch; and they consider those restrictions beneficial. Why then do they not feel any hesitation in demanding unrestricted political rights?

When a people are unable to carry on their business on the capital of their own power, they spend their days in fear and beggary, praying other people and the gods and the planets to help them out of every difficulty. The best description of this is found in the old Mangalakavyas of Bengal. Chand Sadagar was a man of high ideals, and he had to acknowledge defeat, after having suffered much, at the hands of a deity whom he considered low and unworthy of being obeyed. The deity represented a power that was contrary to knowledge and righteousness, was as despotic as terrible, and demanded abject submission. This conception of the ruler of the universe was related to the character of the political regime of those days, as we learn from the Prelude to the Chandi poem by Kavikankan. There was no inviolable law in those days, no justice, no legitimate means to resist the oppression of the strong. The land belonged to the possessor of brute force; the only ways open to the weak were flattery, bribery and, as the last resort, escape. There was a semblance between the social and political conditions of the time and the prevailing conception of the deities.

Yet the Upanishads spoke one day of a providence that is just, orderly and everlasting; prescribed from enternity for eternity; and not subject to the caprice of changing moments; the reason why every one of us could make it his own through knowledge. The more deeply we possess it the further we shall go after overcoming ever-new obstacles. Rightly to know this just and everlasting providence is science. The power of science has given Europe the confidence to assert that it will destroy malaria and other diseases, and banish from human homes ignorance and poverty; that every child will grow up healthy and strong in body and mind; and that complete harmony will be established in the political sphere between individual liberty and general good.

In a spiritual sense India said one day that ignorance is bondage, knowledge is deliverance, and we free ourselves by attaining truth. What is untruth? It is to know oneself as integrally separate. To realize one's unity with the entire universe, to merge the individual soul into the universal soul, is to know truth. We cannot even conceive today how wonderful it was for the ancient Indians to bring so great a truth to the reach of the human mind.

Fundamentally similar to the deliverance sought by ancient India in the spiritual sphere is the deliverance that modern Europe is trying to attain in the material sphere. Here, too, ignorance is bondage, and knowledge deliverance. The truths of science are leading the human mind from isolation to universality, and linking individual power to universal power.

In India the age of the *Rishis,* men who renounced the world to devote themselves to spiritual pursuits, passed in course of time and was followed by the Buddhist age. India kept apart from life the great truth it had learnt, and declared renunciation to be the indispensable condition of deliverance. As a result, there took place in our country a mutually agreed division between knowledge and ignorance, and they have since remained separate, but side by side, like estates legally partitioned by a wall. The world might wallow in narrowness, coarseness and stupidity, the followers of the highest truth would not protest against it and would even support it. Sitting under a tree, the wise man would say, "He alone has attained truth who has seen himself in all and all in himself," and the worldly man would immediately melt in devotion and fill the wise man's scrip with gifts. Sitting in his hall the worldly man would say, "The fool who does not keep people as far away as possible from himself courts disaster," and the wise man would bless him and wish him a long life. This is why there has been no resistance to our ever-increasing apathy and inertness, why for hundreds of years we have been so insulted and defeated in the realm of action.

Things were just the opposite in Europe. Truth was pursued there in the fields of both theory and practice, and the people got together to discuss and correct, in the light of the truth, any flaws that were found in their political and social organizations. The power and the freedom conferred by the truth were thus shared by all, and gave hope and courage to all. Unobscured by the mist of religious rites and incantations, the truth grew in the open daylight, and helped all to grow.

The insult we endured for hundreds of years in the world of action manifested itself to us in the form of political subjection. Just as our hand is drawn to that part of our body which is sore, so our mind is drawn to the political organization set up by the European who has become our ruler. Oblivious of everything else, we are fixing all our attention on having our say in the government of India, and we are refusing to carry out arbitrary orders imposed from above. Authority becomes a burden when it has to be carried on one's shoulders, so we want it to be put on a trolley which we can push with our hands.

Today the whole world is resonant with the cry that man should no longer be ruled by a foreign power entirely in its own interest. In adding our voice to that general cry we have been true to the spirit of our age. Had we failed to do so, and accepted permanent political subjection, we would have humiliated ourselves most abjectly. It is a good sign that truth has appeared to us at last, although through a tiny crack.

So I make bold to say that while I acclaim our newly-awakened national self-respect in so far as it is impelling us to go forward, I also condemn it in so far as it is trying to keep us permanently tied to the past like a sacrificial goat tethered to a post. National self-respect is making us turn our face forward to the world and demand political authority, but it is also making us turn our face backward to our country and demand that in all religious, social, and even personal matters we do not move one step against the Master's will. This is what I call the revival of Hinduism. National self-respect is ordering us to perform the impossible task of keeping one of our eyes wide awake and the other closed in sleep.

When, as punishment from on high, our backs received the strokes of the cane, our national self-respect was rudely awakened and we immediately demanded that the cane forests be burnt down, forgetting that there were bamboo forests beside cane forests. The blame is not to be laid on the cane or the bamboo, but on ourselves, on our obeying the Master more than truth, on our ingrained habit of trusting our blinkers more than our eyes. So long as we remain in this state, there will always be canes for us somewhere in the world.

There was a time when in Europe, too, the Church was dominant in all affairs. The European nations began to stride towards self-government only when they had cast off their fetters. The facts that England is an island and the principal seat of the Church was in Rome, gave the English a special advantage and made it somewhat easy for them to deny the authority of Rome. I do not say that the Church retains no power at all in England, but she is now like a high-born lady who has lost her old position in the family since she became a widow. She used to bully, and she lives in a small room on a small monthly allowance. The youngsters pay their respects to her as a matter of old custom, but they no longer obey her. She would have kept them quiet if she had power and authority as before.

England threw off the old lady's yoke long ago, but Spain has not yet wholly done so. At one time Spain rode the seas full sail, and planted its flag on many a foreign shore. But it has now fallen back, because the old lady was at the helm. Spain got off to a flying start but was soon out of breath, because the old lady was always mounted on its shoulders. It was seen panting and wheezing on the day when the Spanish Armada was beaten by England. As in its religious faith, so in its art of naval warfare, Spain was on that day found to be fettered by tradition. The English ships moved as if in complete accord with the moving wind and water, but the Spanish remained hide-bound in orthodoxy. Anyone with the requisite qualifications could be a commander in the English fleet irrespective of his birth, but only the high-born had that privilege in the Spanish.

Today the common people of all European countries, great or small, have acquired the strength to lift up their heads, and the weakening of the blind power of the Church has taught man to respect himself. Countries like Czarist Russia which lacked this respect for humanity degenerated like ownerless wasteland overgrown with weed and thorn. Man has been insulted, oppressed and robbed in such countries by the bailiffs of the present, the sacred books of the past, and by every other instrument of arbitrary authority.

The difference between the spirit and the form of religion, like that between fire and ash, should be borne in mind. When the form becomes more important than the spirit, the sand in the river-bed becomes more pronounced than the water, the current ceases to flow, and a desert is the ultimate result.

The spirit of religion says that disrespect for man confers no benefit on him who insults and on him who is insulted, but the form of religion says that failure to obey scrupulously the detailed rules for treating man with cruel contempt is apostasy. The spirit teaches us not to destroy our own souls by inflicting unnecessary suffering on our fellow creatures, but the form warns parents that it is sin to give food and drink on specified days of the month to their widow daughter even to relieve her of the worst suffering. The spirit tells us to atone for evil thoughts and deeds by repentance and by performance of good deeds, but the form prescribes bathing in particular rivers at the hour of solar or lunar eclipse. The spirit advises us to cross seas and mountains and develop our minds by seeing the world, but the form puts an expiatory ban on sea voyage. The spirit tells us to revere all good men irrespective of their caste, but the form enjoins respect for the Brahmin, however unworthy. In sum, the spirit of religion leads to freedom, its form to slavery.

There is a certain beauty in religious devotion, and foreign visitors to our country have commented on it, looking at it from the outside like a painter considering the picturesqueness, not the habitability, of an old and ruined building. On my way back from Barisal to Calcutta on the day of the *Snan-yatra* festival, I have seen pilgrims, mostly women, coming to bathe in the Ganges and enduring untold humiliation and suffering at the steamer and railway stations. On a surface view there is a certain beauty in this eager endurance but God, who knows our inmost hearts, does not approve and reward blind devotion of this kind. Bringing up their children hedged in with vows and penances, these women have bowed their heads to everything of this world and knocked their heads against every shadow from the world beyond. Their activity consists in putting obstacles to their free action, and they call it progress to erect sky-high barriers to their real progress. Suffering endured for the sake of truth is beautiful; but then, borne out of blindness or weakness, suffering becomes ugly: it is a reckless expenditure of the heroic power to make sacrifices, which is our greatest god-given asset.

That is the account we are settling today, the debit exceeding the credit. I have seen with my own eyes thousands of pilgrims, both men and women, rushing for a dip in the Ganges in order to earn merit, and when one of them who was ill fell on the wayside and lay dying, none of the others would touch him, since they did not know to what caste the stranger belonged. That, plainly, is spiritual bankruptcy. The very piety of the pilgrims could harden them towards a dying man!

Out of devotion Ekalavya cut off his thumb to give it to the cruel Dronacharya; by that act he simply deprived his own people of the chance to learn the art of archery which he had mastered by lifelong effort. Stupid and futile devotion of this sort is not received kindly by God, because it insults His gifts to man.

He who has been trained to walk with his eyes closed will not be sure-footed if he walks with his eyes open. A born slave who only knows how to lay down his life for his master cannot sacrifice himself for a just cause of his own accord, as if he were his own master.

The perennial misery of our villages is due to the fact that all welfare work was done simply under the inducement of earning merit. Candidates for such merit, if not God Himself, still carry the responsibility of looking after the village; all the others would rather die of thirst than dig one spadeful of earth with their own hands. The village folk have remained as they always were—children in the arms of the "old lady" who has predetermined everything for every man and woman: everything relating to their caste and tribe, their spiritual and material pursuits, their rights and wrongs, and even whether they would lie down or sit up. We cannot really blame them, because the old lady has put their mind to sleep by drugging it with opium. But the wonder is that educated men of today, even young university students, adhere to the cult of the old lady. To see India carried on the hip of its immemorial nurse fills them with satisfaction. From so exalted a position India's feet do not touch the ground, they proudly say, and nothing could be so beautiful as the spectacle of India holding in its hand the sceptre of self-government while still on that hip.

However that may be, there is no doubt that poverty, hunger, and all other emissaries of death are using our homes as their lairs. When they get ready to spring, and plant their fangs on our necks, we find we have no guns—our social rulers forbid the grant of licence for weapons with which we could fight those evils, just as our Government prohibits the guns with which we could protect ourselves from tigers and robbers. Knowledge, reason and intelligence are the weapons with which to scare off those evils. People with unshakable faith in the old lady's rule protest that those weapons are not totally prohibited—we are free to study science, and apply its principles as far as practicable. But then, the strict regulations regarding the licence are calculated to discourage their use. There are too many restrictions, and severe penalties for the slightest infringement. So numerous are the gurus and priests, the charms and amulets, the classical dicta and vernacular proverbs, claiming our careful attention and reverential observance, that in the event of an attack by a bandit we find the bandit a lesser trouble than the gun we have never used.

Kind people who say, "May the chains on your feet be everlasting" as a blessing should also say, "Walk with the feet of other people by climbing on their shoulders." These people would repair and fortify all our old social barriers and personal taboos, and call it renaissance; and they would take pride in the stagnation of life and the cramping of intellect that would follow. They should be told that they must also be prepared to take charge of the millions whom their action would render destitute and hungry. No one, however able, can serve at the same time two interests that are opposed. These people would first smash up all the utensils for fetching water that a thirsty person had, and then they would keep on to-ing and fro-ing between the house and river, trying to fetch him water in a sieve.

The view held by many that the miserable condition of our country is mainly due to foreign rule needs careful examination.

Alliance between the power of the ruler and the power of the ruled is the fundamental principle of English politics. In England this principle has ever carried on a bitter struggle against absolutism, and the story of that struggle has not been kept hidden from us. We learn it openly at Government schools, we pass examinations in it, and it can never be taken away from us. It is the soil in which all our political organizations, such as the Congress, are rooted.

Just as our right to European science lies in the very nature of that science, so our right to English politics lies in the very nature of that politics. A small number of Englishmen might say that it would be better not to give Indian students the opportunity to learn science, but science itself would put those Englishmen to shame by inviting, in a stentorian voice, everyone, of whatever colour or creed, to grow strong by studying it. In a similar way a small, or even a large number of English politicians and journalists might say that it would be better to put all sorts of obstacles in the way of Indian self-government, but English politics would reject that advice by inviting every Indian, of whatever colour or creed, to assert his right in the government of his country.

We shall be sharply told that we are unfit for English political institutions, as sharply as when the Brahmin of ancient India told the Sudra that he had no right to the higher pursuits of intellect and spirit. The Brahmin had built up the division of right very firmly from bottom to top, taking care to cripple mentally the Sudra he wished to cripple physically. A man's activities are like the branches of a tree, and they wither if his intelligence, which is like its roots, is crippled. After the Brahmin had done the not very difficult job of axing the Sudra's roots, his head came down of itself and rested at the Brahmin's feet. But the English have not shut the door of knowledge on us, although it is the main gate to freedom. I expect many English officials regret it, and I notice in them a tendency to go slow on education, but they will never be able completely to forget that to sacrifice one's humanity to self-interest is almost to commit suicide.

If we can hold on with all our might to the idea that our just claim to self-government is inherent in the mental make-up of the English, we shall then find it easy to endure much suffering, and make many sacrifices, for its realization. But if we lapse into our debilitating habit of leaving everything to the unalterable will of the Master, the deep frustration that will result will show itself in two ways: in hole and corner conspiracies leading to sudden outbreaks of terrorism; or in whispered small talk about so and so being a good or a bad Viceroy, about nothing good happening to India while so and so remains in the Viceroy's Executive Council, about the lucky day that will dawn for India when Mr. Morley becomes the Secretary of State for India, and other such matters. In short, the frustration will either pervert our power and drive it underground, or fritter it away in the futilities of small talk.

But I shall not lose faith in humanity, or lack the assurance that in English politics morality is an even greater truth than power; although I am daily confronted with evidence to the contrary, and find the English given to selfishness, love of power, greed, anger, cowardice, and pride. These faults of the English hurt us only because we have them ourselves, because we too are easily frightened and easily tempted, and bear in our hearts envy, malice, and distrust. But if we are great and heroic; generous, virtuous and trustful; and if we possess the greatness which our enemy possesses, we shall then win, morally if not physically and in spite of the injuries caused by our enemy's faults. It is our own cowardice that makes us underestimate the merits of the British Government and overestimate its faults. When there are two parties to a transaction, their combined strength leads to success. By his humble acceptance of the Brahmin's domination the Sudra dug the deep pit for the Brahmin's downfall. The weak are as powerful enemies of the strong as the strong of the weak.

Resistance to injustice is not a matter of brute force, but of moral power arising from a sense of duty. To save the country from perennial police persecution many strong and courageous men are needed, men who will expose it over and over again, and prove it with their lives. I know that even the lowest police officer is more than a man, is a great power, and the Government will spend thousands of rupees to defend a police spy who is being tried in a law-court. Metaphorically speaking, the spy will be given a Government steamship to take him across the rough sea of the trial, while the poor complainant will have to swim, with not even a piece of driftwood to which to cling. It is as if the Government were to tell the persecuted in so many words, "My dear fellow, if you have been beaten up, it will be better for you to die without a protest. Then you cannot be beaten up again." Prestige! She is an old acquaintance of ours. We have met her as the Chandi of Kavikankan's poem, and as the Manasa of the Behula poems. She is above justice and virtue, above everybody and everything, and we must worship her if we do not want every bone of our body to be pulverized. So let us chant:

> *To the Goddess who resides in the*
> *Government as Prestige,*
> *We bow, We bow, We bow.*

But this is ignorance, this is illusion. It is not true even if it appears to be so to the outer eye. The real truth is that the government represents the people, and is greater than all the government officials put together. The real power of the British rests on this truth. Their power is also our power. They also lose the truth if we lose it. If we are so cowardly as not to have faith in the morality of British politics, then the police will continue to oppress, and the magistrates to find it difficult to administer justice; the goddess Prestige will continue to demand human sacrifice; and British rule in India will continue to travesty the essential British way of life revealed throughout history.

The answer to what I have just said will be as follows:

> "The principle that morality is a greater truth in politics than force is all right in theory, but dangerous

> in practice. So the alternatives we are left with are the hard way of secret conspiracy or the soft way of absolute silence under the teeth and claws of the Press Act."
>
> "There are difficulties, of course. Yet we must prove that what we know to be true in theory is true also in practice."
>
> "Our own people will witness against us through fear and greed."
>
> "Right. But truth must still be followed."
>
> "Tempted by praise or reward, our own people will stab us in the back."
>
> "Right again. But truth must still be followed."
>
> "Can you really expect so much?"

Yes, we must expect so much, not one iota less. We will make our demand on the government, but it will not be granted unless we make a bigger demand on ourselves. I know that men are not strong, and the majority of them are in fact weak. But in every great country many are born every day who are the representatives of all mankind. These men bear on their backs the burden of the world's ills, and carve with their hands the path that all will take. They preserve their faith in humanity against all opposition and they keep awake in the deepest darkness of frustration, awaiting the sunrise in the east. Despite the taunts of unbelievers they loudly declare: *svalpamapyasya dharmasya trayate mahato bhayat*—even a little virtue at the centre delivers us from much fear at the circumference. So we shall not bow to fear, we shall bow to morality wherever it can be found in politics. We believe in virtue, and we shall risk our lives to pursue it.

After one hundred and fifty years of British rule we have just been told that the people of Bengal have not the right even to cast a sigh of pain at the misdeeds of the Government of Madras. Until now we had always been told that, under undivided British rule, Madras, Bengal, the Punjab, Maharastra, and all other Indian provinces had been united in both their internal and external aspects; and that the proud achievement of this unity was the kohinoor on the crown of the British Empire. In the West at this moment Englishmen are feeling that the woes of Belgium and France are their woes, and they are marching to lay down their lives in the battle-fields of Belgium and France. At such a moment will the principle hold good in the East that the people of Bengal have no concern with the weal or woe, happiness or misery of the people of Madras? Should we meekly obey such an order? However loudly it may be roared out, we definitely know that there is behind that order a great shame born of misdeeds; and we must match that secret shame with the open charge of our manhood. The English are bound to India by truth; they have come to this eastern country bearing the responsibilities of European civilization. We too shall abide most honourably by that deed, and never let the English say that they undertook the long journey by sea to make mincemeat of India.

Wealth acquired by a nation is meant to be shared with other nations, and a nation really deprives itself if it keeps all its wealth to itself. Science, nationhood, and democracy are the chief wealth of Europe, and the great task of imparting it to India is the heaven-ordained royal mandate of British rule. We also have the task of reminding our rulers about that.

The English might appeal to their own history, saying, "It cost us much effort to build up democracy, and many revolutions to realize its greatness." I admit this. The leading nations of the world have severally discovered different aspects of truth, and each of those discoveries was preceded by many mistakes, much suffering, and many sacrifices. But the nations who enjoy the benefits of those discoveries do not have to travel the long road of those mistakes, sufferings, and sacrifices. I have known Bengali students go to America and master, in both theory and practice, the science of making locomotives. They did this in the space of a few years, but they would have had to live longer than Methuselah if they had to go through all the historical stages of the science of the steam engine beginning with the boiling of the kettle. European science grew on its native soil under the sun and the shower, the wind and the storm, of many ages, but it did not take long to transplant it to the Japanese.

If it indeed be true that we lack gravitas in our character and behaviour, that is all the more reason why we should have authority. If you start with the assumption that so and so has nothing, you will never discover that he has anything. Granting us self-government, the British will open up the path by which we shall discover new powers within us; withholding it, they will make us the permanent laughing-stock of the world, and will prove themselves our worst enemies. A man who is confined within such a small room that he knocks his head against the walls if he but takes a step or two to right or left, can never cherish the noble aspiration of proving his greatness in every walk of life.

I know that at dawn of a new day in history the light spreads to the west, north, and south as soon as the sun rises in the east. If the rate of progress were no faster than one inch for one step, no nation could achieve its end even in infinite time. The British tell us that a country would be free only after it has become completely fit for freedom: no country in the world should be free today if that were true. They vaunt their democracy! The common people of Europe have many serious flaws, but I do not want to speak about them. If a dictator were to order that those people should have no democratic rights so long as they had those flaws, not only would the flaws remain, but the only natural means of removing them would be taken away.

We do not wish to hide, nor should we succeed in hiding, the many flaws that there are in our social and personal lives. But we demand self-government just the same. If in my room I have four lamps, one in each corner, the fact that one lamp is burning low does not deprive me of the right to light another. The important thing is that I shall have light, from any lamp in any corner. In humanity's great festival of lights no "nation has yet been able to light all its lamps, but the festival is going on. Our own lamp went out sometime ago, and all we want is to relight it from England's lamp. This should cause no ill feeling; it would not dim England's lamp and it would make the festival brighter.

There are reasons for hope and they lie both in Britain and in ourselves. I respect the people of Bengal and I know that our young men will not try for ever to appear wise by putting on the borrowed mask of age. I have also known among the English many great-souled men who are intent on bringing to India the ambrosial fruit from the tree of English history. On our side, too, we need men of valour, prepared to accept punishment from the government and ridicule from their own people, and eager to prove their manhood by overcoming the fear of failure.

The ever-young, ever-wakeful God of India is calling to our soul. Immeasurable and unconquerable, our soul has an inalienable right to the land of immortality, although it is now hiding its face in the dust, under the insults of blind social custom and blind political authority. The God of India is calling to us to know ourselves through every blow. He deals us, and every affliction He sends us.

Today we see clearly how large is the world of man, how great the history of man; and in man we see revealed the *Bhuma,* the Supreme Being. Mounted on the chariot of power. He is travelling the royal road of eternity, undeterred by disease or distress, danger or death. Universal Nature has put her garland round His neck. The light of knowledge is shining on His high forehead, and He is being welcomed by an aubade from the summit of the far-off future. The Bhuma is seeking to enthrone Himself in my heart, and in the hearts of all of us, weary though we are with premature age, cowardly with self-distrust, and bent and bemused under the burden of falsehood.

This is no day for squabbling among ourselves in petty jealousy and petty malice, no time for scrambling like beggars for small power and small prestige. This is no day for deluding ourselves with the false pride that struts and swaggers in the dark corners of its own little home, but is ridiculed and disgraced before the great assembly of the world. To derive self-satisfaction from traducing others is the entertainment of the weak, and we shall have none of it. This is the day for censuring ourselves for the many faults whose accumulated weight has crushed our manhood and numbed our reason, for sweeping aside with all our power the refuse that has piled up through many centuries. The greatest obstacle to our going forward lies behind us; our past has flung its bewitching dart at our future. The dust and dry leaves it has raised are darkening the morning sun of our new age, and it is sapping the vitality of our new-stirred youth. We must ruthlessly break free of our past, taking our place among those men and women all over the world who are ever-progressing, ever-alive, ever-wakeful, and ever-seeking. These men and women are the right hand of *Visvakarma,* the architect of the universe. The road they take in their untiring pursuit of truth is bright with the light of knowledge, and every country in every age echoes their triumph.

Afflictions have poured on us like incessant *sravana* rain and caused within us a dark impurity which must be expiated. But how to expiate it? By welcoming the afflictions as the sacred sacrificial fire which will burn away our sins, our ignorance and our inertness. So let us invoke the Supreme God and offer Him, not our lowliness, but the great and immortal god who is within us. Let us pray the Supreme God to call our god to the right of His throne. May lowliness be ridiculed, servility humiliated, and stupidity reproved and banished for ever.

—1917

7

CITY AND VILLAGE

When the bee first made its hive, its main object was food. But when bees banded together to gather honey from many flowers and stored them up against inclement seasons, they also found in the hive their community. This had not merely the mathematical feature of numbers but also the moral aspect of mutual service.

That which begins thus in the enjoyment of the many, ends in the renunciation of the many. Work for all takes the place of work for self; thc individual life finds wider scope in the life of the community. So does one transcend the actual and realize the yet-to-be. Even the effort that fails to be fruitful in one's lifetime is not lost. The community becomes a common ground where relations are extended from the self to others, from the present to the future. And food, becoming abundant, transcends its materiality and expresses a spiritual value, revealing the infinitude of *Anna Brahma.*

In the primitive age men wandered alone, each in pursuit of his precarious livelihood. Their temper was fierce, their habits predatory, their behaviour unsocial. As, on river banks, food became plentiful, communities took form and cvivilizations were born.

Tilling the alluvial soil, men grew rich crops, year after year. They began to see that individuals could gain much more by mutual aid than by trying to deprive one another. With the food problem solved, the social instinct inherent in the nature of man was stimulated. When, at the invitation of the Earth-Motner, men sat down to feast together, their isolated lives found a basis of brotherhood through their common food.

The realization came that in union there was not advantage alone but also satisfaction. For its sake the individual would accept suffering and even death. The Earth gives us food in such a way that it gladdens our eye and enraptures our mind. The golden sunlight, flung from sky to sky, finds a response in the golden harvest from horizon to horizon. This splendour makes man think not only of his meals, but of festive rejoicing.

In the storehouse of the Earth there is, above the provision for our hunger, the nectar of joy. Lakshmi, the Goddess of Plenty, is beautiful as well as benign. The fruit tempts us not merely with its nutriment, but with its form, sweetness and fragrance. As the fruits of the Earth are beautiful, so also is the fellowship of man. The food we eat in solitude may have nourishment, but the food that we eat in fellowship has, in addition, loving-kindness. In such a feast of hearts the utensils become elegant, the serving decorous, the viands refined.

Dearth cramps the hospitality of man, on which society is founded. That is why villages had to grow on the threshold of the Earth's store of food. It was through his re-unions that the immortal in man has expressed itself: his morality, his literature, his music, his art, the variety of his ceremonials. It was through these that he began to be conscious of his own depths, and the ideal of his own perfection became manifest to him.

With the growth of the villages evolved the town. There became focused the forces of government—forts for soldiers, emporiums for merchants, colleges for teachers and students in their pursuit of knowledge, centres of commerce and communion with the outside world. There the soul is encased in hard stone, living is arduous, force contends with force. There the individual seeks to grow at the expense of others. So long as it is not carried to extremes, all this has value. If individuality be suppressed overmuch, man cannot attain fullness of stature. The young forest tree gets stunted if it is smothered under a profusion of undergrowth. On the other hand, the volcanic fire of individual ambition forces up the level of the masses. The standard of achievement is heightened. Competition enhances the output of energy. There is ever-fresh creativity in the fields of knowledge and work, and the sphere of wisdom is enlarged by the influx of the cultures of diverse peoples and countries. And so in the town, where the pressure of the community is relaxed, the individual mind gets a chance to rise superior to the low uniformity of the mass mind—"rustic" is everywhere a synonym for the mind's narrowness.

In their natural state—that is, when the community does not incline too much to one side--the village and the town have harmonious interactions. From the one flow food and health and fellow-feeling. From the other return gifts of wealth, knowledge and energy. A civilization which comprises mainly village life cannot advance very far. There the individual is unimportant, the community predominant. There we have, not the divine warrior, Kartikeya, on his winged steed, but King Demos—pot-bellied, elephant-headed Ganesha. On the other hand, where the town pre-dominates, the individual is all-powerful, the community negligible. There civilization burns itself in its own fires; the more brilliant its flame, the blacker its fuel, until at last it is reduced to ashes. Many civilizations have thus been destroyed by preying on themselves. It is yet too early to say that the civilization of modern Europe is not of this self-exhausting type.

The town is a point where activities are concentrated. The vital forces of our body are gathered at various centres. In the lower types of life these centres are not organized; with evolution, the brain, the lungs, the heart and the stomach gain in their functions. These may be compared with towns.

Towns are organized centres for serving the special needs of the body politic. Of old, machines played a minor role in fulfilling those needs. The joy of creation was the chief motive for manufacture, not the hunger for results.

In the modern age the machine has not only multiplied working capacity but also the hunger for gain and the scale of profit. That is why there is disharmony between the interest of the individual and the community, leading ultimately to conflict. Greed severs the relations between town and village. The town has become a drain on the village because it has ceased to make its contribution to the village. The artificial lights of the town are ablaze—lights that have no connection with sun, moon or star— but the humble lamps of the village are dead. The siren of the factory lures men away from the peaceful refuge of their community. And man is fast reverting to his primeval forest instincts. The individualism of those days has come back to life, but with a new, gigantic stature.

In the beginning, men had grouped themselves in villages to gather and store for mutual benefit. Now they have crowded together in much larger numbers, but each one is the centre of his own accumulation and enjoyment. So, in place of social regulation has come a more rigorous police rule. The solidarity of fellow-feeling has been replaced by the more stringent pressure of a complex system of laws. Where self-gratification is thus exclusive, we are either our own slaves, or slaves of others—in either case slaves. The work that has no room for voluntary renunciation is but a bondage. As an ever increasing number of people get tied together by necessity, with no internal bond of relationship, rivalry and malice rear their heads higher and higher.

The task before us today is to make whole the broken-up communal life, to harmonize the divergence between village and town, between the classes and the masses, between the pride of power and the spirit of comradeship. Those who rely on revolution to achieve this end seek to curtail truth in order to make it easy. When they are after enjoyment, they shun renunciation; when they incline to renunciation, they would banish enjoyment from the land and subdue man's mind by cramping it. What we, of Visva-Bharati, say, is that the nature of man is denied if truth is not offered to him in its wholeness. From this deprivation comes his despair and his ailments.

The factory may be an instrument of much wrongdoing, but it is not a thing that we can reject. The machine is also an organ of our vital force. If our hands have committed robbery, the remedy does not lie in cutting them off: they must be purged of their sin. To try to improve ourselves by crippling ourselves is a counsel of cowardice. All the powers of man seek development and expansion. From the earliest times man has sought to make tools. No sooner had he discovered a new secret of Nature than he tried to capture it with the help of some machine and make it his own. It is in this way that his civilization has advanced.

The day man first drew out the fertility of the soil by making the plough, a hurdle was removed from the path of his progress. This not only revealed the source of his food, but also illumined an obscure chamber of his mind. When he first devised the spinning wheel and the loom, they not only enabled him to cover his nakedness, but also roused the sense of beauty which was to possess so much of his life. If, today, man's body is clothed, so is his mind. The Kingdom of Man depends on this dual clothing.

If any *sanyasin* would plead that this extended commerce with the outside world should be restricted, then he must begin by an indictment of man's pair of hands. And the extreme sanyasin does go to that length. He allows his arms to wither by his ascetic practice of keeping them perpetually uplifted, in a gesture of denial of the world, asserting that he has attained freedom. To restrain man's hands with the command, *Thus far you shall go and no further,* is equivalent to this cult of uplifted arms. Who has the right to lay down such an injunction, to cripple man's God-given powers by saying that he shall not advance as far as the World-worker calls upon to do? We can regulate the exercise of power to ensure our welfare, but we must not bar the way to its expansion.

In the old days man applied his plough and loom, his bow and arrow, his wheeled vehicles, to the purpose of life's progress. So today should modern machines be made to serve the needs of humanity. It is true that because of the machine one rich man is served by thousands; but this only proves that one man can acquire the strength of thousands with the help of the machine. The power thus attained should not be monopolized by the few; it should be used for the benefit of the many. Let not power be concentrated to keep men apart. Let it never be irresponsible.

Civilization has grown by the conjunction of man's intellect with the gifts of Nature. These two must always work in partnership. Whenever the acquisitions of the intellect are hoarded in some strong-room, the store goes on dwindling. We cannot live long on the accumulations of a bygone age.

This new power of man must be brought into the heart of our villages. It is because we have omitted to do so that whichever way we turn there is the picture of penury and defeat. Everywhere our countrymen are crying, "We have failed." From our dried-up hollows, our fruitless fields, our never-ceasing funeral pyres rises the wail, "We have failed." If we can possess the science that gives power to this age, we may yet win, we may yet live.

The ups and downs produced by the inequality of wealth are healthy only within a limited range. No great civilization is possible in a country divided by the constant interruption of steep mountains, as they retard the natural flow of communication. Large fortunes and luxurious living, like the mountains, form high walls of segregation. They produce worse divisions in society than physical barriers.

Some people believe that the solution is to be found in the abolition of the idea of property. But we have to remember that the urges which have created private property are rooted in human nature. If you have the power, you may abolish private property, but you cannot change human nature.

Property is a medium for the expression of our personality. If we look upon the negative aspect of personality, we see in it the limits which separate one person from another. And when, in some men, this sense of separateness takes on an intense emphasis, we call them selfish. But in its positive aspect, it is the only medium through which men can communicate with one another. If we seek to kill our individuality because it is apt to be selfish, human communion itself will lose its meaning. If, however, we allow it to develop, then being creative by nature it will fashion its own world. Most often and for most men, property is the only framework for the creation of a personal world. It is not just money or furniture. It represents not merely acquisitiveness, but also our taste, our imagination, our faculties, and our desire for self-sacrifice.

Through this symbol of our personality we receive, we give, we express. Our highest social training is to make our property the richest expression of the best in us, of our individuality whose greatest illumination is love. As individuals are the units that build the community, so property, when it is alive to its functions, is the unit of wealth that makes for communal prosperity. Wisdom lies not in destroying separateness of units, but in maintaining the spirit of unity in full strength.

When life is simple, wealth does not become too exclusive. Individual property then readily admits its duties to the people. But with the rise in living standards property changes its aspect. It shuts the gates of hospitality, which is the best means of social intercommunication. It displays itself in extravagance. It begets rigid class divisions. In short, it becomes anti-social. With material progress, property has become intensely individualistic: the method of gaining it has become a matter of science and not of social ethics. It breaks social bonds; it drains away the sap of the community. Its unscrupulousness plays havoc.

The forest-fire feeds upon the living wood from which it springs, till it is completely exhausted along with the fuel. When a passion, like greed, breaks loose from the barrier of social control, it acts in the same way and feeds upon the life of society; and the result is annihilation. It has ever been the object of the spiritual training of man to fight those passions that are anti-social and keep them chained.

There are insects in our fields which, in spite of their depredations, leave a surplus for the tillers of the soil, and it does not pay to try to exterminate them. But when some pest that has an enormous power of self-multiplication attacks our crop, it has to be dealt with as a calamity. In human society, in normal circumstances, there are a number of causes that make for wastage, yet we can afford to ignore them. However, the blight that has fallen today on our social life and its resources is disastrous, because it is not restricted to limited regions. It is an epidemic of voracity that has infected the total area of civilization.

We all claim the right to be extravagant in our enjoyment to the extent that we can afford it. We feel ashamed if we are not able to spend as much on individual gratification as our rich neighbour. The tyranny of respectability leads us to ruin.

There is a continual stress on the idea of convenience and comfort. The actual results fall short of the energy spent because of the wastage involved. The shrieking advertisements, which constantly accompany the increase in production, mean an enormous waste of material and life force.

Civilization has turned into a vast catering establishment. It maintains constant feasts for a whole population of gluttons. The intemperance which could have been tolerated in a few has spread to the multitude. The resulting universal greed is the cause of the meanness, cruelty and lies in politics and commerce that vitiate the whole human atmosphere. A civilization with an unnatural appetite must feed on numberless victims, and these are being sought in the parts of the world where human flesh is cheap. The happiness of entire peoples in Asia and Africa is being sacrificed to provide fastidious fashion with an endless train of respectable rubbish.

What in the West is called democracy can never be true

in a society where greed grows uncontrolled and is encouraged, even admired, by the people. In such an atmosphere a constant struggle goes on among individuals to capture public organizations for their personal ends. Democracy is then like an elephant whose one purpose in life is to give joyrides to the clever and the rich.

Under such conditions the organs through which public opinion is formed together with the machinery of administration are all openly or secretly manipulated by the prosperous few. They have been compared of old to the camel, which can never pass through a needle's eye—the gate that leads to the kingdom of ideals. Such a society is callous and cruel to those who preach their faith in spiritual freedom. In such a society people are intoxicated by the constant stimulation of what they call progress, a progress which they are willing to buy at the cost of civilization itself, like the man for whom wine is more attractive than food.

Villages are like women. In their keeping is the cradle of the race. They are nearer to nature than towns, and in closer touch with the fountain of life. They possess a natural power of healing. It is the function of the village, like that of women, to provide peoplc with their elemental needs, with food and joy, with the simple poetry of life and with those ceremonies of beauty which the village spontaneously produces and in which she finds delight. But when constant strain is put upon her, when her resources are excessively exploited, she becomes dull and uncreative. From her time-honoured position of the wedded wife, she descends to that of a maid-servant. The city, in its intense egotism and pride, remains unconscious of the hurt it inflicts on the very source of its life, health any joy.

In the Sanskrit poem, *Meghaduta,* we follow the path of the cloud messenger and in imagination pass over the old-world towns with their beautiful names. We feel that these towns expressed more than anything else the love and hope of man. They treasured some of the splendour of his soul in their houses and temples with the auspicious decoration daily executed by the women, and even in the picturesque bartering that went on in their market-places.

We can imagine what Delhi and Agra must have been in the time to which they belonged. They manifested the creative and human aspect of a great empire. Even in their decay these cities retain the glory of man. But modern cities merely offer opportunities, not ideals.

Cities there must be in man's civilization, just as in higher organisms there must be organized centres of life, such as the brain, heart, or stomach. These never overwhelm the living wholeness of the body; on the contrary, by a perfect federation of their functions, they maintain its richness. But a tumour in which the blood is congested is the enemy of the whole body upon which it feeds as it swells. Our modern cities, in the same way, feed upon the social organism that runs through the villages. They appropriate the life stuff of the community and slough off a huge amount of dead matter, while making a lurid counterfeit of prosperity.

Thus, unlike a living heart, these cities imprison and kill the blood and create poison centres. When men come together only for some material purpose, they form an aggregation but not a congregation, so that there is moral decay. This is the result of true civilization being substituted by what the West calls Progress. I am not against progress but if, for its sake, civilization is ready to sell its soul, I would rather remain in a primitive state.

In India we had for ages our family system. Large and complex, each family was a miniature society in itself. I do not wish to discuss the question of its desirability. But its rapid decay in the present age points to the nature and process of the principle of destruction which is at work. When life was simple and its needs normal, when selfish passions were under control, such a system was quite natural and happy. The family resources were sufficient for all, and no individual member made an inordinate claim. But such a group cannot survive when the personal ambition of one member begins to clamour for more than he needs, when the desire for exclusive advantages runs contrary to the common good. Brothers must then separate and even become enemies.

Goethe's Germany was considered poor by Bismarck's Germany. The standard of civilization, illumined by the mind of Plato, or by the life of Asoka, is perhaps scorned by the proud children of modern times. But are those who lived then to be pitied by the adolescents of the modern age, who have more of the printing press, but less of the mind?

I often like to imagine that the moon, being smaller in size than the earth, produced life on her soil earlier than the earth. Once, the moon too had her festivals of colour, music, movement; her storehouse was perpetually filled with food. Then, on the moon, a race was born that began greedily to devour its surroundings. It produced beings who had an excess of animal spirit coupled with intellect but lacked the imagination to realize that the mere process of addition does not create fulfilment; that acquisition because of its largeness does not produce happiness; that movement does not constitute progress merely because of its speed; that progress can have meaning only in relation to some ideal of perfection. Their plunder soon outstripped nature's power of recuperation. Their profitmakers created wants that were unnatural. They dug deep into the stored capital of nature and ruthlessly exploited her resources. When they had exhausted the limited supply, they fought among themselves for the lion's share. In their scramble they laughed at moral codes and took it to be a sign of racial superiority to be ruthless in the satisfaction of their desires. They exhausted the water supply, cut down the trees, reduced the surface of the planet into a desert riddled with pits. They made its interior a rifled pocket, emptied of its valuables. Like a fruit whose pulp has been completely eaten by insects which it sheltered, the moon at last became a lifeless shell, a universal grave for the voracious creatures who had consumed the world in which they had been born.

My imaginary selenites behave exactly in the way that human beings are today behaving on this earth. Mother

Earth has enough for the healthy appetites of her children and something extra for rare cases of abnormality. But she has not nearly enough for the sudden growth of a whole world of spoilt and pampered children.

Man has been digging holes into the very foundations, not only of his livelihood, but also of his life; he is feeding upon his own body. The reckless wastage is best seen in the villages, where the light of life is being dimmed, the joy of existence dulled, the threads of social communion snapped. It should be our mission to restore the circulation of life's blood into these maltreated limbs of society; to bring to the villages health and knowledge; wealth of space in which to live; wealth of time in which to work, rest and enjoy; respect which will give them dignity; sympathy which will make them realize their kinship with the world of men, and not merely their subservient position.

Streams, lakes and oceans exist not for the hoarding of water exclusively in their own areas. They send up the vapour which forms into clouds, so that there is a wider distribution of water. Cities have their function of maintaining wealth and knowledge in concentrated form. They should do so not for their own sake alone; they should be centres of irrigation; they should gather in order to distribute; they should not magnify themselves, but should enrich the entire commonwealth. They should be like lamp-posts, and the light they shed must transcend their own limits.

Such a relationship of mutual benefit between the city and the village can function only so long as the spirit of co-operation and self-sacrifice is a living ideal in society. When some temptation defeats this ideal, when selfish passion gains ascendency, a gulf is formed and goes on widening. City and village then stand as exploiter and victim.

We have started in India, in connection with our Visva-Bharati, the work of village reconstruction. Its mission is to retard the process of racial suicide. If I try to give you the details of our work, they will look small. But we are not afraid of this appearance of smallness, for we have confidence in life. We know that if it represents the germinal truth that is in us, it will overcome opposition and conquer space and time. We believe that the problem of unhappiness, rather than of poverty, is the greatest problem. Wealth is a synonym for the production and collection of things and men can use it ruthlessly. They can crush life out of the earth and flourish. But happiness, though it may not compete with wealth in its list of materials, is ultimate; it is creative; it has its source of riches within itself.

Our object is to try to flood the silted bed of village life with the stream of happiness. For this scholars, poets, musicians and artists have to collaborate and offer their contributions. Otherwise, they too must live as parasites, sucking life from the people and giving nothing in return.

Most of us who try to deal with the problem of poverty think only of a more intensive effort of production. We forget that it brings about a greater exhaustion of materials as well as of humanity. It gives to the few excessive opportunities for profit at the cost of the many. It is food which nourishes, net money; it is fullness of life which makes one happy, not fullness of purse. Multiplying material wealth alone intensifies the inequality between those who have and those who have not, and it inflicts so deep a wound on the social system that the whole body eventually bleeds to death.

II

What I had to say I have said many times before, and left nothing out. I had strength then, and the current of my thoughts was unimpeded. Age and ill health have now impaired my strength and you should not expect very much from me any more.

It is after a long time I am here. Some of you I do see from time to time—and all I can give you now is my presence and company. When first I bought this house I had no special plans. This much I had thought: Santiniketan was far from crowded life, and while it helped its students also to pass examinations, it gave them something more than the ration stipulated by the Education Department.

But another current flowed in my mind. Living in the villages of Shelaidah and Patisar I had made my first direct contact with rural life. Zamindari was then my calling. The tenants came to me with their joy and sorrow, complaints and requests, through which the village discovered itself to me. On the one hand was the external scene of rivers, meadows, rice-fields, and mud huts sheltering under trees. On the other was the inner story of the people. I came to understand their troubles in the course of my duties.

I am an urban creature, cityborn. My forefathers were among the earliest inhabitants of Calcutta and my childhood years felt no touch of the village. When I started to look after our estates, I feared that my duties would be irksome. I was not used to such work—keeping accounts, collecting revenue, credit and debit—and my ignorance lay heavy on my mind. I could not imagine that, tied down to figures and accounts, I might yet remain human and natural.

As I entered into the work, it took hold of me. It is my nature that, whenever I undertake any responsibility I lose myself in it and try to do my utmost. When I once had to teach, I put my whole heart, into it and it was a great pleasure. Setting myself to unravel the complexities of zamindari work, I earned a reputation for the new methods I evolved; as a matter of fact, neighbouring landlords began to send their men to me to learn my methods.

The old men on my staff grew alarmed. They used to maintain records in a way that I could never have grasped. Their idea was that I should understand nothing more than what they chose to explain. A change of method would create confusion, so they said. They pointed out that, when it came to litigation, the court would be doubtful about the new way the records were kept. I persisted, though, changing things from top to bottom, and the result proved to be satisfactory.

The tenants often came to see me—for them my door was always open, day and night. Sometimes I had to spend the whole day listening to their representations, and meal-times would slip by. I did all this work with enthusiasm and joy. I had lived in seclusion since boyhood and here was my first experience of the village. I was satisfied and heartened and filled with the pleasure of blazing new trails.

I was anxious to see village life in the minutest detail. My duties took me to distant parts by river, canal and waterways, and here was a chance to see the changing panorama of life. The everyday tasks of villagefolk and the varied cycle of their work filled me with wonder. Bred in the city, I stepped right into the heart of rural charm and filled myself with it. Then, slowly, the poverty and misery of the people grew vivid before my eyes and I began to wish that I could do something for them. I was struck with shame that I was a zamindar, impelled by the money motive, absorbed in revenue returns. Since that realization I awoke to the task of trying to stir the minds of the people, make them shoulder their own responsibilities.

To try to help villagers from the outside could do no good. How to kindle a spark of life in them—that was my problem. It was so difficult to help them because they did not have much respect for themselves. "We are curs," they would say; "only the whip can keep us straight."

One day a fire broke out in a village nearby. The people were so utterly dazed that they could do nothing. Then the men from a neighbouring Muslim village came rushing and fought the fire. There was no water and thatched roofs had to be pulled down to stifle the flames. The stricken ones had to be beaten up before they would let this be done. You have to use force in order to do good! And then they came to me saying, "What luck that our roofs were dismantled—that is how we have been saved." They were happy that the beating benefited them; but I was filled with shame at their submissiveness.

I planned to put up a small building for them at the centre of the village, where at the day's end they could get together, read newspapers, listen to the Ramayana and

Mahabharata—it would be a sort of club. For, I had been unhappy, thinking of their cheerless evenings; it was as if the same tedious line of a verse was being endlessly sung. In course of time the building was erected. But, then, it was never used. I engaged a teacher, but the pupils kept away with all kinds of excuses.

In contrast, the Muslims from the other village came to me and said, "Will you give us a teacher? We are ready to bear the expense." I agreed and a school was set up in the village and probably it is still there. In my village, nothing could be done, its inhabitants had lost all faith in themselves.

The habit of dependence has come down to us from time immemorial. In the olden days one rich man used to be the mainstay of the village and its guide. Health, education and all else were his responsibility. I have praised that system, but it is also true that because of it the common man's capacity for self-reliance was enfeebled.

In my estate the river was far away and lack of water was a serious problem. I said to my tenants, "If you dig a well, I shall get it cemented." They replied, "You want to fry fish in the oil of the fish itself! If we dig the well you will go to heaven through the accumulated virtue of having provided water for the thirsty, while we shall have done the work." The idea, obviously, was that an account of all such deeds was kept in heaven and while I, having earned great merit, could go to the seventh heaven, the village people would simply get some water. I had to withdraw my proposal.

Let me give another example. I had built a road from our estate office up to Kushtia. I told the villagers who lived close to the road, "The upkeep of this road is your responsibility. You can easily get together and repair the ruts." It was, in fact, their ox-cart wheels that damaged the road and put it out of use, during the rains. They replied, "Must we look after the road so that gentlefolk from Kushtia can come and go with ease?" They could not bear the thought that others should also enjoy the fruits of their labour. Rather than let that happen, they would put up with inconveniences.

The poor in our villages have borne many insults, the powerful have done many wrongs. On the other hand, the powerful have had to do all the welfare work. Caught between tyranny and charity, the village people have been emptied of self-respect. They ascribe their miseries to sins committed in previous births, and believe that, to have a better life, they must be reborn with a greater fund of merit. The conviction that there is no escape from sufferings makes them helpless.

Once upon a time the rich regarded it as an act of merit to provide water and education. Through their goodwill the villages were well off. But when they started to move away to towns, the water-supply ceased, malaria and cholera struck hard, and the springs of happiness dried up in village after village. It is hard to imagine a life as cheerless as in our rural areas.

I could see no way out. It is far from easy to do something for people who have cultivated weakness for centuries and do not know what self-help means. Still I had to make a start. In those days my only helper was Kalimohan. Fever used to grip him morning and evening. With my medicine box I treated him myself, and never thought that I could get him to survive.

The shastras say: *Shraddyaya deyam*—if you give, then give with respect. That is how I set to work. From my office building I had often watched the farmers going afield with bullock and plough. Their land was in small strips and each man tilled his own holding. That, I knew, was a great waste of energy. So I sent for the men and said, "Plough all your land jointly. Pool the strength and resources of all. Then you can even use tractors. If you all work together, small differences in personal holdings will not matter. Whatever the profit, you will share it equitably. Store all the produce of the village at one place and you will get a fair price from the middleman." They listened and said, "The idea is good, but how to work it out?" If I had the knowledge and the training, I would have said, "I will take the responsibility." They all knew me. But one cannot do good simply by wanting to; there is nothing so dangerous as ignorant help. Young men from town once went to a village to help the people. But the people cried jeering, “Look, there come the quarter-rupee gentlefolk!” No wonder—these young men knew neither the language of the villagers, nor the workings of their mind.

Something had to be done. I sent my son and Santosh abroad to learn agriculture and dairy farming. And in several other ways I started to work and to think.

It was about this time that I bought this house. I thought I would continue here the work I had begun at Shelaidah. The tumble-down house was supposed to be haunted! I had to spend a lot of money on its repair. Then, for a while, I sat still. Andrews said, “Sell off the house.” But I thought to myself, “Since I have acquired it, maybe there is some significance. Maybe one of my two objects in life will be fulfilled here.” How and when? I had no idea. When seed is strewn in an auspicious moment even on barren land, it suddenly sprouts. At that time there was no such sign. Everything was scarce. However, slowly the seed started to put forth shoots.

My friend Elmhirst helped me a great deal. It was he who turned this place into an independent field of work where progress was steady. It would not have been right to lump it with Santiniketan.

I have one more word for you. We must see that a force from within the people starts functioning. When I was writing *Swadeshi Samaj* the same idea had struck me. What I wanted to say then was that we did not have to think of the whole country; we could make a start with one or two villages. If we could free even one village from the shackles of helplessness and ignorance, an ideal for the whole of India would be established. That is what occurred to me then and that is what I still think. Let a few villages be rebuilt in this way, and I shall say they are my India. That is the way to discover the true India.

—1928

8

CO-OPERATION

In every country the poorer classes make a far larger sector than the well-to-do. Then, which countries in particular may be named as poor? It is where the means of livelihood are the fewest and even those are often blocked. Where the "have-nots" can aspire to a better life, hope itself is a real asset.

It is not enough to say there is a shortage of funds in our country; worse, there is a shortage of hope. We cast all the blame on fate as we bear torments of hunger. We grovel in the dust, assured that only the mercy of Heaven or of people from outside can save us. It does not strike us that the remedy is in our own hands.

That is why it is better to instil hope in the heart than to offer alms. It is his own deficiency, and no decree of fate, that makes a man sink into the depths. To think there is no escape from preordained misery is to make the misery perpetual. To seek new paths in a constant renewal of strength—that has always been the secret of progress. When a man waits helplessly for a turning in the wheel of fortune, he has to be regarded as shorn of manhood.

Man loses his true stature when he fails to unite fully with his fellows. A complete man is one who has this capacity for union, a lone individual is a fragmented being. We know that a child dreads ghosts only when he is alone. This is the lone person's fear of his own weakness. Most of our fears are replicas of this fear of ghosts.

There is the fear of poverty. It can be countered if we stand and act in a group. It is only by combining that man has achieved all that is worthwhile in life—knowledge, faith, power, wealth. Sandy soil yields no crop because it does not stick together. Sap cannot collect in that soil but escapes through the interstices. The soil can be made productive by the addition of loam, humus and leaf-mould which close the gaps. It is the same with human beings. Where the chasms between them are wide, their strength is of no use.

Let us examine one of the basic things when we say that man has really found himself by uniting with others. Man can speak, he has language. Animals have no language. Through the unifying force of language a mind, otherwise sunk in itself, combines with others. It is through speech that the mind I have is projected into other minds, and those in turn become part of my own. This thinking in unison is an enrichment that negates inner poverty.

When mankind learnt to preserve language through the written word, the area of contact between minds was extended. Spoken words do not go far. They get lost in course of time, and often become distorted as they pass from mouth to mouth. But the written word crosses oceans and mountains and is still unchanged. Every man may thus gain the thinking of countless others.

That is not all. The written word goes beyond uniting the minds of living men alone; it removes the barriers between the minds of today and the minds of those who belonged to a remote past. This great contact between thoughts has created what is called civilization. What is civilization but a state of union in which the strength of each individual adds power to all and the power of all fortifies the individual?

Behind the abject poverty of our country is the fact that we keep ourselves segregated, trying to bear all our heavy burdens by ourselves. In Europe, when the steam engine came, many handicraft workers were thrown out of employment—how could the bare hands of individuals challenge the machine? But the people of Europe think for one another in a crisis—where civilization is a powerful force, fellow-feeling must be intense. The realization began to grow that the combined efforts of the people could be their strength and their capital. The mind of civilized man has gained in stature by the union of the thoughts of many; likewise, the combined work of many could attain a new magnitude. This union leading to prosperity has been an ever-widening path in Europe and I do not see a better path anywhere else.

I have to visit a small village once in a while. I stand on a verandah, and see field after field stretching away for miles. This land is cultivated by many farmers, some of whom own two bighas, some four and some even ten. The first noticeable fact is that only a few cultivators have the requisite number of bullocks, while others have too few or too many. Ploughing may start at the right time, or it may be late—that has to depend on the farmer's resources. Further, much of the labour of the bullocks is wasted as the direction of the plough changes frequently because of the twisted boundary lines of the plots. If each cultivator did not regard his small holdings as an independent unit, if all adjoining strips were reckoned as one, fewer ploughshares and bullocks could do the tilling and much wasteful labour would be eliminated. There would again be a great saving of energy and expense if, after harvest, the farmers collectively stored and marketed their produce.

He who can do the largest measure of work in the shortest span of time wins out. That is why men employ tools, which make one pair of hands equal to five or even ten. The savage who scratches the earth with his bare hands has to accept defeat from the man with the plough. It is not his own physical strength but the use of tools that has helped man to get the best out of cultivation, transport, and such activities as weaving, extracting oil, and manufacturing sugar. The plough, the loom, the bullock cart, the horse-drawn vehicle and the oil press have all reduced time and increased output. These have made progress possible; otherwise, there would have been but little to distinguish man from the ape.

Man worked with his small tools until the advent of modern machinery driven by steam and electricity. The small tools acknowledged defeat from the big machines, as bare hands had yielded to the hands equipped with tools.

The time has come even for our cultivators to consider these facts; otherwise they cannot survive. But it will not help merely to theorize; the right answers must be found through actual practice. In Europe and America they are all moving fast in that direction. They plough and reap, tie the sheafs and store the crop in granaries, all with the help of machines. Applied to this country, this process will have several advantages. Before cultivation can start, one has often to wait for the rains to come. If there is a brief shower one day, a small plot can be just lightly scratched with the ploughshare; in case there is no more rain for weeks, there will have to be late sowing, and then the unripe crop may get covered with water in the late monsoon. There may be trouble at harvest, too; extra helping hands are scarce in the village and men from outside have to be hired; if there is a heavy downpour while the reaped crop still lies on the fields, heavy losses will follow. With a mechanical plough and harvester, full advantage may be taken of every favourable turn in the weather; cultivation will be completed and the ripened grain gathered with great speed.

These machines, it is true, can be put to work only over large tracts of land, and considerable funds are needed for their procurement and use. But if therefore we give up all hope saying that our peasantry cannot afford them, it will simply mean inviting ruin. In the present age of mechanization our men, cultivators as well as artisans, must accept the machine or step back and further back until they topple into a perilous chasm.

He who is lacking in hope must perish. No one can save him by offering alms or some other help. He must be made to realize that what is not possible for a single individual will be possible when fifty unite in a group. The fifty who have hitherto cultivated their separate holdings, side by side, will have all the advantages of a large working-capital if they pool all their resources—land, labour, granaries. It will not be difficult then to get the machines. A farmer can hardly do good business with a small daily surplus of a seer of milk, but if a hundred men collect all their spare milk, they can produce and sell *ghee* after they have bought a butter-churning machine. In Europe this is a common practice. People in Denmark and other small countries have combined and by the proper marketing of butter, cheese and cream they have eliminated poverty from their lives. Besides, trade contacts have made these farmers and dairymen realize their close kinship with the peoples of the world, and their minds have become enriched with understanding and knowledge.

This combination of many people to earn a living is known in Europe as the co-operative system. It is by this system that our country can be rescued from its age-long poverty and stagnation.

Our educated men are eager to serve the country. Nursing the sick, feeding the hungry and giving alms to the poor—these are some of the ways. That is like trying to put out a fire by blowing on it, when it has enveloped the whole village. Our ills cannot be cured by treatment of the symptoms. The causes have to be removed. First, the people must cease to be parochial; they must feel that they are part of a world society. Secondly, in the economic sphere, their efforts have to be co-ordinated to the efforts of men elsewhere. In other words, like tall trees they need wide spaces to spread out their roots under the earth and their branches in the air and light. Fruit-bearing will then be easy and profuse and no one will have to worry on that account.

II

In a certain phase of civilization the city gains greatly in importance over the village. It is not that the country's life finds a more intense expression in the city; the country's power gets concentrated in the city which thus attains a new prestige.

The social temper of the Bengal village repeated itself to some extent in the life of the city. In outward appearance the city was quite unlike the village; yet at some points the two resembled each other in character. This was the case even with the big cities. With all their pride they recognized their kinship with the village. The two were somewhat like the inner and outer apartments of a house; wealth and pomp resided in the outer section, leisure and ease in the other, and the two were linked by the closest relationship.

It is no longer so. In the last half-century the city has grown to be very much the city and the village cannot reach it even by the back entrance. This is what is meant by the saying: "Your own courtyard is alien ground." Villages lie all around the cities and yet it is as if the two are hundreds of miles apart.

This unnatural severance can do no good. Not that it is something peculiar to our country; it is a mark of the modern age. The wind from the West has scattered the seeds of social dissonance all over the world, destroying not only peace and happiness, but the very core of life itself. Here is a problem on which people everywhere must ponder.

Civilization, as it is known in Europe, sucks up the life of the masses to build a special kind of power. It is like the flowering of the bamboo—the flower draws the life of the whole plant. The English word for this is exploitation. The smaller part seeks to grow big by swallowing the larger. The small becomes bloated while the large is drained of sustenance. The result is a growth in the intensity of an anti-social, separatist individualism.

I have suggested already that the might of a country is in its cities even though the villages are its life centre. It is in cities that ways have to be devised for the development of financial, political and democratic power. These ways are not always social in character. Here the machine has more importance than human values. All power goes to those who control the machine. Therefore, cities are in the main a competitive field and here the urge for mutual help is not suitably encouraged.

Individualism and competition are necessary for the generation of power, but danger comes when the proper limits are exceeded. Modern civilization has indeed gone beyond the limits. Many-limbed as it is, a multiplicity of appurtenances are needed for its expression and preservation. Inadequate resources are almost a crime in this order of life which has to stand on a vast assortment of materials. Education, health, law and justice, communications, transport, food, accommodation, conduct of warfare, maintenance of peace and order—all cost huge sums of money. Poverty brings with it humiliation, for poverty is a drag on the progress of this civilization.

Money is now the source of all power and is prized above all else. Even State policy is no longer based on the extension of sovereignty; what is more attractive is the expansion of trade and commerce, the means of making new wealth. In the days when civilization was not many-limbed, the scholar and the sage, the hero and the philanthropist were more highly respected than the rich. By the honour shown to them, it was humanity itself that was honoured. People were contemptuous of the mere money-maker. All civilization is now a parasite of wealth. It is not merely the earning of money, the worship of money is dominant. The false god destroys the goodness in man. Never before was man such a great enemy of man; for, nothing can be more cruel, more iniquitous, than this gold hunger. The all-powerful hunger is a product of modern civilization, and measures for satisfying it surpass all other endeavours.

Out of greed comes sin and sin leads to destruction. Greed is an anti-social impulse. All that weakens the social sensibility of man leads at every step to internal conflict and does not let the fire of discontent die out, until the very social existence of man is violently disrupted and must come to its end.

A ceaseless clash goes on in the western world between those who make big money and those who are mere tools for the purpose. There is no visible way of settling the conflict; for, the greed of the working class equals the greed of the capitalist. Everyone wants more and more money to enjoy in full measure the bliss of civilization. To hope that the tussle will come to a stop somewhere seems futile.

When greed and the worship of might grow unrestrained in social life, it becomes impossible for man to devote himself to the development of his humanity. He longs for power, not for fullness of self. Under such conditions the city becomes supreme and the village falls into neglect. All opportunities, all advantages, all that is needed for the enjoyment of life pile up in the city; the village simply slaves to provide food and just manages somehow to exist. Society gets divided—on one side there is light and on the other deep darkness. It is thus that urban civilization in Europe tears apart the integrity of mankind. Ancient Greece was centred on cities, with a water-tight division between the master and the slave. So, after a hey-day of prosperity, Greece was swept aside. Ancient Italy, too, was city-based and for a time she wielded great power. Power is intrinsically a-social—it creates a rigid class distinction between master and slave. The few masters become parasites of the numerous slaves. This parasitism destroys the basis of their humanity.

The West has created areas of light and darkness not only in its own regions but throughout the world. Its demands, vast as they are, cannot be met within its frontiers. The people of Britain must have India in their possession in order to acquire and maintain the wealth which is said to be essential for civilized living. If they give up India, they will have no option but to lower their high standards of luxury. They must have slave peoples as their instrument of power. That is why the entire British race lives as India's parasite. That is why the Great Powers of Europe have been anxious to carve out Asia and Africa for themselves; otherwise their pleasure-ridden civilization would have to be half-starved.

The resources needed for unlimited enjoyment cannot be equitably divided among all. Many must be deprived, that a few can go on adding to their hoarded wealth. Here is the most crucial problem for the peoples of the West. Within their own countries greed has brought about the same rift between the Haves and the Have-nots as exists between subject races and their foreign overlords. This extreme dissonance is hostile to the religion of universal humanity. Wherever the unity of man is in peril, disruptive forces arise, openly or in secret. The master hurts the slave openly, but covertly the slave hurts even more, for he destroys the moral sense in his master. This is a great danger; for while animals die only from lack of food, man dies also from lack of moral sense.

In Aesop's Fables we read of the one-eyed deer that was killed by an arrow coming from its blind side. The purely material aspect of the current civilization of man is his blind side. We find in Europe today a large and varied co-operation in the acquisition of knowledge but a bitter competition in the acquisition of wealth. A single lamp of knowledge in Europe kindles a thousand lamps and the light of all illuminates the modern age. Thus Europe towers over all the other continents. Convener and priest of the worship of knowledge, she has collected many faggots from many places to feed the sacred fire so that it would never be quenched. Never before in the history of man have co-operative principles in the realm of knowledge been so widely at work. In earlier times every country developed its learning independently and in isolation from others. The learning of Greece belonged mainly to Greece, the learning of Rome to Rome, and it was the same in India and China. Happily for the countries and regions of the European continent, they are closely situated and the natural boundaries between them are not so difficult to cross—there are no barriers of vast deserts or high mountain ranges. They are one in religion and for a long time this religion was centred on Rome.

For many centuries while learning was disseminated all over Europe through the medium of only one language, Latin, the oneness of religion worked further for unity. The basic principle of this religion is unification; at its centre is the love of Christ and its injunction is service to all mankind. In course of time each country as it came out of the nursery of Latin began to advance scholarship through its own language. All learning, however, flowed through a single channel and was stored in one treasure house. Out of this was born western civilization, a civilization of knowledge rooted in co-operation. We speak of eastern civilization, but that is a negative term, merely implying that it is not European. There is no concord between the minds of China and Arabia; in many respects they are even contrary. The Hindus of India and the Semitic races of western Asia are quite dissimilar in their culture. The absence of co-operation in the learning of the Asian nations has led to their ancient history being split into different sections. Under the compulsions of history some areas may have had cultural exchanges but the mind of Asia never became a unified entity. So it is that, when we speak of eastern civilization, we are thinking only of our own national civilization. That is why Asia, unlike Europe, has been unable to make a strong impact on the modern age.

But where is it that, in this civilization of Europe, the seed of its doom is being sown? It is in its failure to co-operate in the realm of material progress. Here the countries of Europe are separated and mutually opposed to an unnatural extent. As material progress, aided by science, becomes vast and varied, curious contradictions arise. On one side there is the rapid advance of life-saving knowledge—never before did man have such mastery over his physical health, over the productivity of land, and over all material obstacles to living. It is as if man is trying to snatch from heaven the nectar that gives deathlessness. On the other side, we see something entirely contrary. Never before has there been such devoted effort to deal out death; every country in Europe is most enthusiastically engaged in this effort. Europe grew powerful by unifying knowledge; it is now ready to utilize that very power to destroy itself. In its search for knowledge

Europe advances on the path of saving life, while in its search for material wealth it marches on the path of destroying life. It is difficult to foresee which force will ultimately prevail.

Some say that, to avert disaster, the machines now employed by man should be scrapped. That is absurd. Quadrupeds have four feet but no arms. They somehow manage to do what is needed for a bare existence. This bare existence means poverty and defeat. Man, however, is fortunate in having been provided with two hands, which add vastly to his efficiency, an advantage that gives him mastery over all other living beings. When he increased his efficiency further, with the help of machines, he took one more step forward. It is absurd to suggest that this power of man should be curbed. Nations who have failed to gain control over the machine must face defeat, just as beasts had to face defeat from man.

The problem arises when one man, or a group of people, aided by some opportunity, captures the means and materials of power. There was a time when all political power in every country was in the hands of one man, whose will alone prevailed. When he had to be restrained from misuse of power, an appeal to his conscience was the only way. But the ears of the mighty were not always open to such appeal. So it happened that people in some countries wrested authority from the ruler by force. They said, "The power of the ruler is simply the sum total of our own power. The concentration of power in one hand has made us powerless. If we can find out how each one of us can use that power, then by the union of all our power we can have our united kingdom." England had this opportunity. If it did not come to several other countries, that was because all nations do not have the education or the mental capacity to divide up the concentrated power and then unite it anew for application in practice.

This is also true of the power of money, restricted to a particular class. It is by collecting in their own hands the working capacity of many people that the rich attain their position. Their capital is the combined labour power of many people and it has taken concrete shape in wealth. That labour power is the real capital, the power inherent in every worker. If they can only say, "We shall combine our strength," their real capital will be in their own hands. Those who lack the capacity to unite must of necessity suffer. They can gain no permanent benefit by abusing others or by robbing them.

In material affairs man has for long neglected his humanity, using his strength only in the furtherance of greed. Numberless slaves are harnessed to the chariot of wealth and driven forward under the whip. The oppressed must eventually say to themselves, "It is our divided strength, concentrated in the hands of the mighty, which has given them power. By attacking the power we can break it but we cannot put it together again, and so it will be no good to us. We must, therefore, try to combine all our labour power and thereby gain economic benefits to be shared by all."

That is the co-operative principle. It is this principle which has made man great in knowledge and given a moral basis to his conduct of practical affairs. Where it is lacking, there is suffering, malice, falsity, barbarity and strife.

The clash of power against power raises conflagrations on all sides. Man is being sacrificed at the altar of individual greed. Unless stopped, this will cause the most terrible havoc in history. The rift between the mighty and the weak in the world of material affairs is the most serious danger today. Differences exist between the learned and the ignorant; but men do not raise walls of separation over the right to knowledge; the intellectual classes are not anxious to gain strength by group combination. The inordinate greed for money, however, has been raising walls to keep people apart in every country and in every home. Differences also existed between people in the past; but the walls did not reach such great heights. Greed did not overwhelm and corrupt all literature, art, politics and domestic life. Beyond the monetary fields were other wider fields where men could unite.

It is not the rich but the poor who must rescue society from the crushing weight of great wealth. The building of an entrance gate to the heavily barred economic field must lie in their hands. The weakness of the poor has so long kept civilization weak and incomplete; they must set this right by the conquest of power.

The co-operative principle is progressing in European countries, who have an advantage over us—they have more experience and sense of combination. We Indians, especially the Hindus, are backward in this respect. But it may well be expected that even we, goaded by our unbearable poverty and by our great longing for a better life, will ultimately accept the co-operative way. If we fail, there will be no escape from our woes and no one can be blamed on that score.

It has been said that poverty will be rooted out if our living is reduced to bare necessities, as in the past. That simply means that one who is lying right at the bottom cannot fall further down. It is hardly a solution.

The history of man does not indicate that he will ever retrace his footsteps. His intelligence has to express itself in newer creations through the ages. New times make new demands. Those who cannot meet the demands get dismissed. By his inventive power man goes on creating new opportunities for himself, and his needs multiply. Even before the ploughshare came, man existed on fruits and roots which he gathered from the forests. No one at the time could have felt that he lacked anything. When the plough was invented, cultivation began and there followed trade and commerce, laws and regulations. Trouble also came in its wake—violence, theft and robbery, forgery, cheating and lying. But to suggest that the plough should be discarded on this account is to ask that we should face backward while we try to march. History tells us of some races who, instead of advancing on the path of newer creations, remained stationary, their faces turned to what ancient possessions they had. They were worse than the dead, because they were dead-alive. It must be conceded that the dead do not need money to spend; is that any reason to say that the best solution of the problem of poverty is death? It is not for man to continue somehow to exist with the relics of past ages. Man's needs are varied;

his necessities are numerous; but he has also the ability to meet his own demands.

What is a luxury? Should we say that it is a luxury to give up the castor oil lamp for the kerosene lantern, and to replace the kerosene lantern with electric light? Only if we have no use for artificial illumination, once daylight is gone, can we think of giving up electric light. That light is only an improved way of satisfying the need which was felt when darkness fell and the bean oil lamp was lit. It is no luxury today if we use electric light, and not to use it is only a sign of poverty. When the bullock cart was first devised, it was an expression of wealth; but within it lay concealed the conception of the motor-car. If the man who used the bullock cart does not ride a motor-car today, it is only his poverty that is indicated. The wealth of one time is merely poverty in a succeeding age. Only the feeble-minded may suggest that poverty will be conquered if you revert to it.

That most of the advantages created in the modern age are enjoyed only by a few, while the majority are denied, is a misfortune for which society must expiate. The remedy lies not in restricting wealth or taking forcible possession of it or giving it away. The remedy is in stimulating in all people the capacity for creating new wealth; in other words, it is in expounding to the people the principles of co-operation.

I do not believe that inequality in wealth can ever be completely removed by force. The disparity inherent in man is sure to assert itself. There is also the difference in temperament. Some love to hoard money while others have no such inclination, so that unevenness in wealth is created. A mechanical uniformity is neither possible nor even desirable. As in the world of nature so in the world of man, complete uniformity paralyzes initiative and makes the intellect idle. But excessive unevenness is equally bad, since it greatly hinders the development of social contact amongst people by the creation of distance between them. Evil builds its nest under the shadow of such barriers.

Every man is entitled to adequate wages and leisure. To have only the barest means of living is an insult. The dignity of civilized living rests today on a chosen few, maintained by the unwilling labour of many. Vast masses of people, deprived of education, health and the means of enjoyment, are doomed to exist as dullards. We have seldom worried about the consequence, but we cannot remain unconcerned any longer. All over the world today violent social upheavals have started, symptoms of intensification of power within a narrow space. That power must now be released; it must become broad-based.

At one time the co-operative principle was followed to some extent in our village-based economy. But life now is not as simple as in those days. Besides, it is now far more difficult for the rich to be selfless. So much the better, though; the masses must now develop their own inherent strength—that will be of more permanent worth. If the Indian economy is based once more on co-operation, the villages which are the nurseries of our civilization will be vitalized and the whole country will gain a new life. Poverty holds the scene and there are as yet few towers of accumulated wealth standing as barriers on the path of the humble masses. So co-operation will have little challenge to face. And it is my earnest prayer that the liberation of wealth, its re-distribution, be carried on in this country to the fullest extent, so that, through the united efforts of all the people, the goddess of food and plenty may be firmly enthroned for all time to come.

—1929

The Morning star whispers to Dawn,
"Tell me that you are only for me."
"Yes" she answers, "and also
only for that nameless flower."

Rabindranath Tagore

9

THE CHANGING AGE

In those days not too far behind, our countryfolk used to while away their free hours in small groups in the temple pavilion, gossiping and playing cards, and they had little to think or talk about beyond the familiar orbit of rural life. Their cultural needs were met, off and on, by a wandering theatrical party who performed folk-plays, by readings from the ancient epics, and poets' verse-making contests. The theme came inevitably from the store-house of legendary lore. Here was an intimate world of narrow horizons, rotating on its own axis; year to year, generation to generation, its substance was changeless, repetitive. Beyond it, in the wider world, there went on the ceaseless making of history, not deadened by sacred injunctions and rigid custom. The history changed its content perpetually by the conflict and interaction of one part with another, giving rise to ever-new problems. All those processes, however, were well beyond the range of our mental vision.

The first onslaught on our walled-up complacency came with the Muslim occupation of the land. But the Muslims too were of the unchanging East and prisoners of their own past. By the might of arms they built an Empire, but their mind had no creative exuberance. When they had settled within our borders, they came into sharp and frequent friction with us, but a friction that was external, one set of inflexible ways in conflict with another. Their influence dug deep into our administrative system but failed to reach the region of the mind. Persian came to be widely used by the higher classes and some of its vocabulary was absorbed into the Bengali language itself. Yet Persian learning left few visible marks on the Bengali literature of the time—its themes and insights bear no trace of Muslim literary tradition. The only exception was Bharatchandra's *Vidyasundar*—in its sophisticated diction and sustained cadence it has intimations of the mild irony of Persian lore.

So, on Indian soil, two civilizations, each hemmed in by its own fixed beliefs, stood side by side with averted faces. It cannot be said that they did not react on each other, but that happened in a very limited measure. Muslim physical prowess impinged on the land with terrific force, yet it could not rouse the people into stirrings of thought or creative enterprise. A further point to note is that, even though the Muslims came dashing into Hindusthan from the world beyond, they failed to make our vision reach out toward that world. Having built their settlements they closed the gateway by which they had entered. Even if, once in a while, the gateway yielded to new onslaughts, nothing much happened that could make us turn to the world outside. That was why we still viewed narrow horizons from the pavilions of our rural shrines, content with the familiar gossip and card games.

Then the British came. They came not simply as men but as the symbol of the new spirit of Europe. The British advent is a strange episode in our history. On the personal plane these newcomers remained farther away from us than the Muslims, but as emissaries of the European spirit they made a contact with us wider and deeper than that of all their predecessors. The dynamism of Europe made a vigorous assault on our stagnant minds—it acted like the torrents of rain that strike into the dry under-earth, give it vital stirrings and bring forth new life. There had been the same kind of dynamism in the immense surge of the Renaissance washing out of Italy, overflowing the whole Continent. Its rich, varied effects were nowhere regarded as hurtful to national prestige. Receptive minds must absorb the richness of new thought; the cross-currents of give-and-take flow fast at the points where the intellect is alive and awake.

The spirit of the modern age has cast its radiance from the western horizon, illumining the entire span of world history. The mind of Europe, under some tremendous urge, has projected itself into every corner of the earth. Where-ever it has gone it has made conquests. And what is the secret of its power? The answer is to be found in the integrity of its pursuit of truth. It has not been deluded by intellectual lethargy, illusive fancy, superficial resemblances, or the echoing of the age-old wisdom. It has sternly controlled the easy temptation to accept what instinct urges man to believe. It has not tried to adapt truth to the needs of individual thinking. With stern avowal of reason, with freedom from personal bias, it has annexed new areas to its domain of knowledge, day by day.

Here in India we are still conditioned by our surrender to the fatalism of the almanac, but there are gaps in our walls through which the European spirit has forced itself to our inner yard. It has brought us the great gift of knowledge in its universal aspects. It has wakened us to the all-pervasive inquiry of the intellect, keenly seeking to probe into the innermost nature of whatever is near at hand or far away, whether big or small, whether of practical or of theoretical value. It has demonstrated that knowledge is indivisible and one unbreakable thread runs through all phenomena. For it, no prevalent dictum, even if hoary with age and sanctity, can override the testimony of even the least of natural happenings.

As with the physical world, so with the moral. Among the doctrines of the new age that have come to us is the one that makes all men equal before the Law. Whether a Brahmin kills a low-caste Sudra or a Sudra kills a Brahmin, it is murder all the same, and calls for the same punishment.

No ancient injunctions in this regard can sway the scales of justice.

Revolutionary changes have come in our thoughts and attitudes. This is evident in the proposition that those whom social usage has decreed to be untouchables should be given the right to enter temples. There is still a section of the orthodox who seek to justify the temple entry of the casteless on scriptural sanctions, and not moral grounds; but such lop-sided advocacy makes little impression. The inner voice of the people has begun to tell them that neither the scriptures nor tradition nor the force of personality could set a wrong right—the moral standpoint alone counted.

To return to the Bengali literature of the Muslim time, we see there the idea that unlimited right to do wrong is a mark of supreme power, an idea that even besmirched the concept of the divinities. The ruthlessness which men of might employed to consolidate their power was an instrument also for the gods and goddesses, and their worth was indeed measured in terms of their capacity for striking terror. It was for the common man to obey laws and conventions; he who stood on a pedestal had the unquestioned right to break every law. The reckless arrogance of unlimited power carried an attribute of godliness. The current saying in those days was, "The Lord of Delhi is as the Lord of all creation," both sharing the same right, not of the ready dispensation of justice but of the arbitrary exercise of might. The Brahmin was called *Bhudeva,* divinity on earth, and that was merely a claim of supremacy with no corresponding nobleness that divinity might suggest. Ethics had no place there. The old codes of law sanctioned as inviolable the Brahmin's birth-right to perpetrate wrongs on inferior castes.

Though the British Empire is far more powerful than die Mughal, even an idiot would not today claim for Lord Willingdon that he was the equal of the Lord of all creation. The terrible power to eliminate entire villages by aerial bombardment fails to strike us as an attribute of the divine. And while we suffer under British rule, we judge it by the common standards of decency applicable to all, and do not hesitate to demand proper conduct from the mighty. The fact is that by accepting the common norm of right and wrong the British Empire has, at one point, placed itself on the same moral plane as the weakest of its subjects.

When we first became acquainted with English literature, we gained from it not only a new wealth of emotion but also the will to break man's tyranny over man. Our ears rang with the proclamation abolishing the shackles of political slavery. And there was the stern challenge to the attempt to turn human labour into an economic commodity. This was a novel point of view. We had taken it for granted that the accident of birth or the fruits of action pursue us from our past lives and could never be disowned; that the resultant sufferings and the indignities of an inferior status had to be meekly accepted; and that our lot could change only through an accident of rebirth. Even today, in our educated circles, there are people who believe in resisting political denials but ask us to be reconciled to the insult of social and religious disabilities. They forget that the habit of submitting to conditions into which one is born as predestined and inevitable is the strongest link in the chain of our political servitude. However, our contact with Europe has awakened us to the universal laws of cause and effect; and it has given us a set of values against which scriptural dispensation and age-old convention declaim in vain. It is on this ground that we take our stand in trying to improve our political status in spite of all our shortcomings. If, today, we challenge our rulers with demands which we would not have dreamed of presenting to a Mughal Emperor, it is because of the ideal voiced in the words of the poet: "a man's a man for a' that."

I have now passed my seventieth year. I stepped into the new age, which may aptly be called the European age, about the middle of the nineteenth century, in a period which the youths of today have sarcastically named Victorian: Britain, representing Europe to us, was then at the summit of power and prosperity. No one could then have thought that there could ever be a crack in her splendid mansion through which ill-luck might enter. Whatever the lessons of history there was yet no visible sign anywhere that an adverse wind could blow against the western civilization of the time. Nothing had happened so far to reduce the value of the ideals of freedom of speech and individual liberty, ideals over which the battles of the Reformation and the French Revolution had been fought. In that Victorian age the United States was torn in a civil war for the liberation of the Negro slave. That age echoed with the messages of Mazzini and Garibaldi. Gladstone thundered forth his condemnation of the Turkish atrocities. That was also the time when we in India began to nurse the hope of our country's freedom. In that hope, it is true, there was an antagonism to the British conqueror; but there was also a vast faith in the British character. How else could we have come to the conviction that on grounds of human decency we could demand equal partnership in India's administration?

The suddenness with which we stepped out of one era into another with its new meaning and values! In our own home, in our neighbourhood and community, there was still no deep awareness of human rights, human dignity, class equality. Amid the contradictions of the day, there was our ambiguous attitude to science. Even while science knocked at our door, the sacred almanac with its star-readings held its ground. All the same, the impact on us of the western cult of reason was real.

So, obviously, the Victorian period was our time of intensive co-operation with Europe. In fact, wherever our mind was not in contact with the mind of Europe, wherever our education was not in key with the European system, the loss was ours. This co-operation was easy so long as our regard for Europe suffered no shock. For, as I have said, it was out of our great regard for Europe that the new age was born. Had we not observed how, in the realm of intellect, Europe paid homage to illusion-free reason and in the realm of practical affairs, stood for the rights of man? It was thus that, in the face of all opposing factors, self-respect grew in us and with it a new hope for our people. We started to judge the mighty by their own lights. It must be admitted that there had been no such ground by which to approach our former rulers; while chance favours might befall us when they felt generous, we could never make any claims on the basis of common ethics, nor as man demanding the warmth of understanding from man.

Since then history has sped on its course. Asia has shown signs of waking from its long night of slumber. Japan has won an equal status with the world Powers by her contact and conflict with the West. She has proved that she lives in the present and not in the twilight of a remote past. And other eastern nations also have stepped into the new epoch. We had hoped all the while that we too should achieve harmony with this phase of world history; that our chariot of self-determination would roll towards progress; and the British themselves would promote the onward movement. But having waited for a long time we now discover that the wheels of the chariot were not meant to move. The British in India believe only in law and order, rules and regulations. Measures to improve education and health are not related to the country's actual needs. There are few openings for the people to produce new wealth. And the future holds no prospects; all our resources are swallowed up in the demands of law and order. It is, ironically, India's link with Europe that deprives her of the great gifts of the time. In the solar dazzle of the new epoch she has to be a mere dark spot.

England, France and Germany are heavily in debt to the United States. But even if the debts were twice as heavy, it would not have been impossible to pay them off, provided the debtor countries only maintained law and order while they reduced their living standards drastically,—food rations cut to half of normal requirements, water supply a fraction of what would quench thirst, education adequate for no more than five or seven per cent of the people, and health services barely touching the emasculation deep in the bones. However, such denials are contrary to civilized life. So the debtors say blandly, "We shall not honour our liabilities." India, taking her stand on the bare decencies of life, could say likewise:

"We shall no longer put up with the bankruptcy imposed by an intolerably expensive system of administration, which weighs upon us as an enormous slab of stone and assigns us to a primitive state." After all, why should Europe restrict to the lost the standards which she herself has formulated? Does it not bear responsibilities towards all the world?

It has become increasingly plain that, beyond the bounds of Europe the torch of its civilization was not meant to give light but to start fires. So it happened that pellets of opium supported by cannon balls were directed at the heart of China, an atrocity the like of which history had not known before, except perhaps in the newly discovered America where European Powers in their greed for gold used deceit and violence to destroy the wonderful *Maya* people. In the Middle Ages the barbarous Tatars raised monuments of human skulls in the lands they overran; the wounds they inflicted healed up, though. The poison that civilized Europe forced down the throats of the vast Chinese masses made a lasting injury. When the youth movement in Iran tried to rouse the country from the spell of its centuries of stupor, civilized Europe put down the brave attempt; the tragic story has been narrated by Schuster in his work *Strangling of Persia*. And everyone is aware of the horrors of European rule in the African province of Congo. Even to this day the Negroes in the United States have to bear heavy social indignities.

Then came the Great War, and all at once a curtain went up on the stage of western history. It was as though a drunken maniac was revealed in all his starkness. Such evil ferocity may have briefly disturbed some long-ago periods in the Dark Age, but never in such a monstrous form. Barbarity in the olden times was like a whirlwind contained in its own dust cloud; but this modern eruption was something volcanic, the repressed criminality blowing the lid off and belching forth lava-like, reddening the sky with its glare and consuming the green richness of the earth. Since that time Europe has lost faith in its own sanity, and in its insolence it begins to mock the very ideal of the universal well-being of man. The Europe we used to know through our association with Britain was reticent about things that were uncouth. Now it makes no pretence of such decency.

Western civilization no longer admits any call to a sense of honour. Inhuman cruelty struts in barefaced pride. We see Europe's best pupil in Asia, Japan, copying in Korea and in China its master's arrogance of might. The crazy brutalities of the Black and Tans in Ireland are beyond the wildest fantasy. Here in India itself we have witnessed the horror of Jalianwalabagh. The very Europe which had once reviled Turkey now flaunts Fascism. The freedom of self-expression which we had once learnt to look upon as Europe's great gift is ruthlessly suppressed. Respect for the individual conscience used to be propagated from the pulpits of Europe; but what has happened to those who believe in the teachings of Christ, who have been bidden to love even their enemies?

Italy punishes its political dissentients with transportation to a penal island and it is well known what hell that stands for. And Germany, in which the light of Europe's culture was at its brightest, has torn up all civilized values—with what ease has an unspeakable devilry overtaken the entire country!

Let me quote a passage from what the French pacifist youth, Rene Reymond, has written:

> So, after the war I was sent to Guina .... Condemned to fifteen years' penal servitude, I have drained to the dregs the cup of bitterness, but the terms of penal servitude being completed, there remains always the accessory punishment—banishment for life. One arrives in Guina sound in health, young, vigorous, one leaves (if one leaves), weakly, old, ill .... One arrives in Guina honest—a few months later one is corrupted .... They (the transportees) are an easy prey to all the maladies of this land—fever, dysentery, tuberculosis and most terrible of all, leprosy.

As the brutality of post-War Europe spreads the world over, we ask ourselves, "Where is that supreme tribunal of man to which the victims of outrage could make their final appeal? Are we to give up our faith in humanity? Must barbarism be answered with barbarism?"

But even in this despondence we must remind ourselves that, however terrible the current degradation, we are still able to pass judgement on it with our heads held high. We can proclaim that it is only worthy of contempt; we can condemn it and say, "Perish!" That there are men in these dark days who would risk life itself in daring to make the challenge is far more meaningful than all the fear and the misery. The batons of the tyrant may break every bone in their bodies and yet they will not say with folded hands as of old, "The Lord of Delhi is as the Lord of all creation!" nor admit that the mighty one can do no wrong. Rather would they declare that the man of power must bear the largest measure of responsibility and, judged by his own standards, any acts of evil that he commits would be the most condemnable. If, ever, the day comes when the oppressed peoples lose the power to drown the growls of raging tyranny with the cry of "Shame!", then indeed shall we know that the new age has spent itself and become hopelessly bankrupt.

—1933

Let not my love be a burden on you,
my friend,
Know that it pays itself.
Rabindranath Tagore

10

WHAT THEN?

An artist carefully selects his lines and colours and harmonizes them in such a manner that they are no longer a sum total of lines and colours. They transcend themselves to form a picture in which the artist's ideal of perfection finds release in concrete attainment. Likewise, Indian in pursuit of her ideals of liberation tried to train and manipulate life's forces towards a deliberate end. Life, according to her, must not only grow within itself but outgrow itself into a higher meaning beyond it, as a flower outgrows itself into fruits. Lines through their discipline of limits lead the form to the region of beauty which is the expression of the limitless. India's aim has been to guide life's current between its boundaries or banks towards an unbounded sea of freedom. The object of this paper is to discuss the principles and methods of such an art of living which once India taught her children to adopt.

The flesh is impure, the world is vanity, and stern renunciation is the way to salvation—that was the ideal of spiritual life held forth in medieval Europe. Modern Europe, however, considers it unwholesome to admit an everlasting feud between the human world of natural desires and social aims on one hand and the spiritual life with its aspiratkms and discipline on the other. According to her, we enfeeble the moral purpose of our existence if we put too much stress on the illusoriness of this world. To drop down dead in the race-course of life, while running at full speed—that is acclaimed as the most glorious death.

Europe, it is true, has gained a certain strength by pinning her faith onto the world, by refusing to dwell on its evanescence and condemning the preoccupation with death as morbid. Her children are trained up in the struggle which, as science says, is for the survival of the fittest. That, Europe seems to think, is the whole meaning of life. But then, whatever the practical value of such a philosophy of living, the fact remains that our connection with the world is far from permanent.

Nature, for its own biological purposes, has created in us a strong faith in life by keeping us unmindful of death. Nevertheless, not only does our physical existence end, but all that it had built up goes to pieces at the peak of achievement. The greatest prosperity dissolves into emptiness; the mightiest empire is overtaken by stupor amidst the flicker of its festive lights. We may be weary of this truism, but it is true none the less. Therefore, all our actions have to be judged according to their harmony with life's background, the background which is death.

And yet it is equally true that, though all our mortal relationships must end, we cannot ignore them while they last. If we behave as if they do not exist, merely because they will not persist, they will all the same exact their dues, with a great deal over by way of penalty. We cannot claim exemption from payment of fare because the railway train has not the permanence of the dwelling house. Trying to ignore bonds that are real even if temporary, only strengthens and prolongs the bondage.

That is why the spirit of attachment and that of detachment have to be reconciled in harmony, and then only will they lead us to fulfilment. Attachment is the force drawing us to truth in its finite aspect, the aspect of what is, while detachment leads us to freedom in the infinity of truth which is the ideal aspect. In the act of walking, attachment is in the step that the foot takes when it touches the earth; detachment is in the movement of the other foot when it raises itself. The harmony of bondage and freedom is the daace of creation. According to the, symbolism of Indian thought, Shiva, the male principle of Truth, represents freedom of the spirit, while Shivani, the female principle, represents the bonds of the material. In their union dwells perfection.

In order to reconcile these opposites, we must come to a true understanding of man; that is, we must not reduce him to the requirements of any particular duty. To look on trees only as firewood, is not to know the tree in its entirety; and to look on man merely as the protector of his country or the producer of its wealth, is to reduce him to soldier or merchant or diplomat, to make his efficiency the measure of his manhood. Such a narrow view is hurtful; those whom we seek to invest with glory are in fact degraded.

How India once looked on man as greater than any purpose he could serve, is revealed in an ancient Sanskrit couplet which may be translated thus:

For the family, sacrifice the individual;
For the community, the family;
For the country, the community;
For the soul, all the world.

A question will be asked: "What is this soul?" Let us first try to answer a much simpler question: "What is life?" Certainly life is not merely the facts of living that are evident to us, the breathing, digesting and various other functions of the body; not even the principle of unity which comprehends them. In a mysterious manner it holds within itself a future which continually reaches out from the envelopment of the present, dealing with unforeseen circumstances, experimenting with new variations. If dead materials choke the path of its ever-unfolding future, then life becomes a traitor that betrays its trust.

The soul is our spiritual life and it contains our infinity within it. It has an impulse that urges our consciousness to break through the dimly lighted walls of animal life where our turbulent passions fight to gain mastery in a narrow enclosure. Though, like animals, man is dominated by his self, he has an instinct that struggles against it, like the rebel life within a seed that breaks through the dark prison, bringing out its flag of freedom to the realm of light. Our sages in the East have always maintained that self-emancipation is the highest form of freedom for man, since it is his fulfilment in the heart of the Eternal, and not merely a reward won through some process of what is called salvation.

That was what had been preached and practised in India. Our sages saw no end to the dignity of the human spirit which found its consummation in the Supreme Spirit itself. Any limited view of man would be false. He could not be merely Citizen or Patriot, for neither city nor country, nor for that matter the bubble called the world, could contain his eternal soul.

A poet of classical India, who was once a king, had asked, "What if you have secured the fountain-head of all desires: what if you have put your foot on the neck of your enemy, or by good fortune gathered friends around you; what, even if you have succeeded in keeping mortal bodies alive for ages—what then?"

That is to say, man is greater than all objects of his desire. You can direct man's life towards perfection if you remember the greatest truth about him—that his life courses from infinite to infinite, without beginning and without end.

It was in this breadth of vision that our ancient sages differed from the European monks of the middle ages, having arrived at a different standard of the value of man's life. The sages of India did not consider relentless effort, up to the very end, to be a matter for glorification. Work was not the be-all and end-all with them; their aim was, rather, to come to the end of ail work. They had no doubt that the liberation of the soul had to be man's greatest quest.

Europe is tirelessly singing paeans to Freedom, which to her means freedom to acquire, freedom to enjoy, freedom to work. This freedom is by no means a small thing. But our sages found no final satisfaction in it, still questioning: "What then?" To them this freedom was not ultimate; for it was their quest to gain freedom even from desire and from action.

In the process of attaining freedom a man must bind his will in order to save its forces from distraction and wastage, so as to gain for it the velocity which comes from bondage itself. Those who seek liberty on a purely political plane must constantly curtail it and reduce their freedom of thought and action to that narrow limit which is necessary for making political liberty secure, often at the cost of liberty of conscience. Are the soldiers of Britain free men, or are they not merely living guns? And what of the toilers in her mines and factories, mere appendages of the machines they work, giving their life-blood to paint red the map of Empire? What percentage of Englishmen actively participate in their political freedom? Europe may have preached and striven for the rights of the individual, but where else in the world is the individual so much of a slave?

The answer to this question leads to the paradox I have stated. Freedom may be attained only through the bonds of discipline, through the sacrifice of personal inclinations. Freedom is a profit which may be gained only if you lay out an adequate capital of self-restriction.

Individualism was also the object of India's quest—not of this narrow kind, however, since it strained towards self-emancipation. While Europe's ideal of freedom has manifested itself in the full rigour of mechanical bonds, the Indian ideal found expression in the strict regulation of all details of daily life. If we fail to see the ideal behind and focus our view on its external manifestations which are of die present age, then indeed in India individual liberty will appear thoroughly fettered. It has happened over and over again in the history of man, that means have got the better of ends. It occurs either when some passion like greed lures our minds away from the ideal end to the material means, making us blind to their relative value; or when through lassitude of spirit our endeavour falls short of its aim and takes pride in conforming to regulations that no longer have meaning, that exact our sacrifices but give us nothing in return.

That is what happened in our country. We still submit to the bondage of all kinds of social restrictions, but the emancipation which was the object is no longer in our view. We have forgotten the ideal, we have lost all sense of the grandeur of our striving, what remains is the impotence of blind habit. If an onlooker concludes that the social system of India is only meant to keep down people by meaningless prohibitions, we may get angry, but we shall find it difficult to refute him.

It is not my object to lament our downfall. What I wish to point out is that India originally accepted the bonds of her social system in order to transcend society, even as the rider puts reins on his horse and stirrups to his own feet, in order to attain greater speed. India knew that society was not the ultimate end of man, but the collective endeavour of individuals was the best way towards liberation; and her bonds were more severe than those which Europe imposed on herself. That was because she had an even greater freedom in view. Her present plight only shows that the deeper the lake, the more cavernous is its hollow when it has dried up.

The Isa *Upanishad* has spoken of this reconciliation of the opposite aspects of bondage and freedom, of the means and the ends.

"In darkness are they who worship only the world, but in greater darkness are they who worship the Infinite alone. He who accepts both saves himself from death by his knowledge of the one, and attains immortality by his knowledge of the other."

That is, we must have our fulness of worldly life before we can attain the Infinite. Desire must be yoked to work for the purpose of transcending both desire and work, and then only can union with the Supreme be contemplated. Mere renunciation of the world does not entitle one to immortality.

The same scripture says:

> "Performing work in this world, must thou desire to live a hundred years. O Man, no other way is open to thee except the way of work."

A rich life of work can alone fulfil the destiny of man. When this worldly life is perfected, it comes to its natural end, and the fetters of work loosen and drop off. As a help to view life and life's ending in this simple, natural way, the *Isa Upanishad* bids us remember:

> "All that is in this world is enveloped by God. Enjoy that which He gives you. Do not covet the wealth of others."

The poison of worldly life is neutralized as soon as we comprehend that it is enveloped by God. Its pettiness is relieved. Its bonds do not get a grip on us. And no room for snatching or grabbing is left, once we accept all enjoyment as a divine gift. This elevation of work and enjoyment by linking them with the Supreme is at the root of the Indian social system. It is thus that India tried to liberate the human soul.

In Europe we see only two divisions of man's wordly life—the period of training and that of work. It is like prolonging a straight line till, wearied, you drop your brush. Such elongation of a straight liiie can never produce a picture; it can have no design, it is meaningless. Work is only a process and cannot really be an end in itself. It must have some gain, some achievement, as its object. And yet Europe has omitted to put before man a definite goal in which work finds its natural termination. To acquisition, whether of material or of knowledge, there is no limit. And European civilization puts all emphasis on the progress of this cumulative acquisition, forgetting that the best which each individual can contribute to the progressive life of humanity is in the perfection of his own life. So their end comes in the middle of things; there is no game, but only the chase.

We also say that desire does not get exhausted, but rather increases, with its attainment. How then is one to come to the end of work? The reply that India of eld gave was that there is an exception to this general rule; there is a point where attainment does arrive at its terminus. The universe cannot be so madly conceived that desire is an interminable song with no finale. And just as it is painful to stop in the middle of the tune, it should be pleasant to reach the final cadence.

India has not advised us to come to a sudden stop while work is in full swing. It is true that the unending procession of the world has gone on, through ups and downs, from the beginning of creation till today; but it is equally obvious that each individual's connection with the world does get finished. Must he necessarily quit it without any sense of fulfilment? Had that been so, he would have been unfortunate indeed.

On the one hand, I represent in me an endless current of generations; with my life I add to its flow, I contribute as much as I can to its store of ever increasing experience of knowledge and possibilities of power. On the other hand, I represent the individual whose life has a beginning and an end in itself and who must reach some ideal of perfection in that limited space of time. The unending stream can have no idea of completeness, its nature is movement. To be its part for a moment and then to vanish, means struggle and no realization. Those who say that the world is a humming top of absurdity which hums and whirls for no reason whatever, should not preach their gospel of work and help this madness of movements. As in the heart of all things there is the impulse of unending progress, so there must also be the ideal of fulfilment which alone gives meaning to all movement. Who is to realize it if not the individual? The movement which is in the finite has its claims on him, but the fulfilment which is in the infinite has also its call to him. When we respond to that call, then death does not come as an abrupt interruption to our world of reality.

So, in the division of man's world-life which we had in India, work came in the middle and freedom at the end. As the day is divided into morning, noon, afternoon and evening, so India divided man's life into four parts, following the requirements of his nature. The day has the waxing and waning of its light, so has man of his bodily powers; and acknowledging this, India gave a connected meaning to his life from start to finish.

First came *brahmacharya,* the period of education; then *garhasthya,* that of the world's work; then *vanaprasthya,* the retreat for the loosening of bonds; and finally, *pravrajya,* the expectant awaiting of freedom through death.

Nowadays we have come to look upon life as a conflict with death—the intruding enemy, not the natural ending—and every stage of our life is marked by that conflict. As the time comes for youth to depart, we try to hold it back by main force. As the heat of desire cools off, we wish to revive it with fresh fuel of our own devising. When our sense organs weaken, we urge them to keep up their efforts. Even when our grip has relaxed, we are loth to give up possession. We ignore all the rest of our life except, its morning and noon. And when at last its gathering dusk forces itself on us, we grow mutinous or despondent. We do iiot recognize the inevitable as natural, and cannot give up gracefully that which has to go—we wait until it is snatched from us. The ultimate fact comes as our worst enemy, since we have lost the capacity to receive it as a welcome guest.

The stem of the ripening fruit becomes loose, its pulp soft, but its seed hardens with provision for the next life. Our outward losses, due to age, likewise have corresponding inward gains. But, in man's inner life, his will plays a dominant part, so that these gains depend on his own disciplined striving; that is why, in the case of indisciplined man, it is so often seen that his muscles slacken, his legs totter, and yet his stern hold on life refuses to let go its grip, so much so that he is anxious to exercise his will in regard to worldly details even after his death. This kind of tenacity is coming to be regarded, even in our country, as something to be proud of; but what is there so glorious about it?

Renounce we must, and through renunciation gain—that is the truth of the inner world. The flower must shed its petals for the sake of fruition, the fruit must drop off for the rebirth of the tree. The child leaves the refuge of the womb in order to achieve further growth of body and mind; next, he has to leave the self-centred security of a narrow world to enter a fuller life which has varied rela-tions with the multitude; lastly comes the decline of the body, and enriched with experience man should now leave the narrower life for the universal life, to which he must dedicate his accumulated wisdom on the one hand and on the other, enter into relationship with the Life Eternal; so that, when finally the decaying body has come to the very end of its tether, the soul views its breaking away quite simply and without regret, in the expectation of its own rebirth into the infinite.

From individual body to community, from community to universe, from universe to Infinity—this is the soul's normal progress.

Our sages, therefore, keeping in mind the goal of this progress, did not, in life's first stage of education, prescribe merely thef learning of books, but brahmacharya, disciplined living, by which both enjoyment and renunciation came equally easy to the strengthened character. Life being a pilgrimage, with liberation in the Supreme Being as its object, the living of it was a spiritual exercise to be carried through its different stages, humbly, reverently and vigilantly. And the pupil, from his very initiation, had to keep this final consummation in view.

The series of adjustments between forces within and without, which constitute the physical life, have become automatic; but in the case of man, his mind comes in as a disturbing factor which is still in the stage of conscious experimentation and which may involve him in endless trouble before its activities can be related to universal law. For instance, the body may have come to the end of its requirement of food for the time, while the mind will not have it so. Seeking to prolong its satisfaction beyond actual need, the mind spurs on the tongue and the stomach to greater effort, upsetting age-long adjustments and making for trouble in the process of procuring needless material.

Once the mind refuses to be bound by actual requirements, there ceases to be any reason why it should cry halt at any particular limit. So, like trying to extinguish fire with oil, its acquisitions only make its desires blaze all the fiercer. That is why it is essential to habituate the mind, from the very beginning, to the conscious need of keeping within the natural limits; in other words, to make it attuned to universal nature, so that, with every liberty to play its varied tunes, it may learn to avoid discord with the Good and the True.

After the period of such education comes the period of worldly life. Our lawgiver Manu tells us:

> "It is not possible to discipline ourselves as effectively when out of touch with the world as when pursuing the world-life with wisdom."

That is, wisdom does not become complete except through the full living of life; and thoughtless discipline is not true discipline, but merely the pursuit of custom, which is only the way of ignorance.

Work becomes easy when desire has learnt to control itself. Then alone does the householder's state become a centre of welfare for society, and instead of being an obstacle helps in the final liberation. When all his work has the detachment of selflessness, its obligations cannot curtail the freedom of his spirit.

The second stage of life having been thus spent, the decline of bodily powers must be taken as a warning that it is coming to its natural end. This must not be taken dismally, as a notice of dismissal to one still eager to stick to his post, but joyfully, as the news of promotion to higher duties.

The field for the exercise of bodily strength, of alert senses and keen desires, must now be left behind. The crops have been harvested and stored and now it is evening, the time to stop work and set out for home, where peace awaits us. Have we not been toiling through the live-long day for this home, the abode of joy? From that joy did we come, to that joy shall we return. Or else, what have we been sweating for?

After the infant leaves the womb, it still has to remain close to its mother for a time, attached in spite of its deliverance, until it can adapt itself to its new freedom. Such is the case in the third stage of life when man, though aloof from the world, keeps contact with it. He still gives the world his store of wisdom, as the ripe fruit dropped from its stem gives food, before its seed finds the soil for a renewal of life. His wisdom comes as a shower of rain which is for all, because it descends from the upper air of disinterested detachment.

Then at last comes a day when even such free relations must end, and the released spirit, its world-work completed, is ready to face the Supreme Spirit.

Only in this way can man's life be truly lived, without having to try conclusions with death at every step and without being overcome by it finally.

This fourfold way of India attunes the life of man to the grand harmony of the universe, leaving no room for unrestrained desires to pursue a destructive course, leading them on to their final relation with the Supreme.

Whatever other way we envisage—Patriotism, Philanthropy, however big the name—it can never lead us to finality, but will leave us in the lurch suddenly, in the midst of our activities, with the question ringing in our ears: What then, what then?

I feel that doubt may arise here: How far is it possible to mould the whole people of a country in this way? My reply is that, when the wick is burning at its tip the whole lamp is said to be lighted. The ideals of life find luminous expression only in the topmost few. If in any country even a small number of its people succeed in realizing an ideal, that is a gain for all the people. If ever the day comes in India when her leading men hold aloft the highest Truth and highest Good above other considerations, and regulate their lives accordingly, then they will give a special direction and power to the efforts of all.

There was a time when the great thinkers of ancient India led such disciplined, purposeful lives in communion with the Supreme, and their spirit was at work not only in religion but in statecraft, warfare, commerce, literature and art. Not only did Maitreyi say, but the whole country was echoing to her cry: *Yenaham namrita syam kimaham tena kuryam?* What shall I do with that which is not of immortality?

If we believe that that voice of protest has been utterly silenced in our country, then complete surrender to the conquering foreigner is indeed the only recourse for us; and that will be far better than futile efforts to bring back the dead to life!

But that is just what we cannot admit. However dire the outward degeneration which has overtaken us in India, there is an inmost core still alive within us, which refuses to acknowledge anything less than the Supreme as the highest gain. Even now, when any great soul strikes a higher note, our whole being responds, unhindered by lesser worldly considerations. Even as we vie in our outward display of loyalty to Mammon, our true soul is not completely lost.

Nowadays, on festive occasions, we often add a foreign brass band to the usual set of our festive pipes, creating a terrible chaos of sound, Nevertheless, through all the clash and clangour, the plaintive Indian note of our real yearning reaches the sensitive ear. While, in the public part of our homes, the foreign big drum and blatant trumpet proclaim the pride of wealth and the emulation of fashion, that deafening din does not penetrate the privacy of our inner life, to drown the auspicious conch which voices the true festivity deep in our hearts. However vociferously we proclaim the efficacy of European state-craft and social customs and business methods, these can-not fulfil our needs; they rather hurt the ideal of the Highest which is still alive within us, and our soul cries out against them.

We were not always this kind of a market crowd, jostling and elbowing one another so vulgarly, quarrelling over prestige and titles, advertising our own worth in unashamed exaggeration. Here is sheer imitation and sham, with no redeeming feature of courtesy or grace. Before this age of make-believe overtook us, we had an inherent dignity of our own, which was not impaired by plain living or poverty. That was for us a congenital armour, shielding us from all the insults and trials of our material vicissitudes. Stripped of that protection, we are driven to take our stand behind bluster and bluff. Dignity has become an outside thing which we must prop up by outward show. We have to hunt for its paraphernalia in foreign shops, and never can we gather together enough of them. And the meaningless excitement of this pursuit, which we have come to look upon as the only happiness, has made us, who were only in partial subjection, slaves of the foreigner all over.

Even so, I believe it has not worked its way into the core of our being. It is yet of the outside and that is why it is so obvious. Not having become really used to our new acquisitions, we make so much fuss over them, like the threshings of an inexpert swimmer.

I still feel sure that if one who is worthy stands before us and proclaims that this insane competition, this ephemeral wealth, this aimless excitement, is not the best for us; that each set of activities has its natural termination; that in the perfection of the ending must be our ultimate fulfilment; and that, short of the Supreme all is petty and futile,—then, even through the clamour of the market-place, the message will not fail to reach our heart. "True! True!" the heart will respond; "there is nothing truer." Then our school-learnt lessons on the profits of insensate competition and the glories of blood-stained nationalism will drop out of our minds and the glitter of armies and the glamour of navies cease to fascinate us.

Moreover, I cannot admit that there is anything in man's higher life which is good only in a particular geographical latitude. It is not true that we must take refuge in meekness because we are weak, or that we want righteousness only as a convenient cloak for hiding our poverty. Ideals preached by the great personalities of the world need for their acceptance more steady courage, perfect training and power of sacrifice than what is needed to make good our school-learnt lessons on the profits of competition and the carnage of a hungry nationalism thriving on human flesh.

To prepare during adolescence for the world-life in which the soul is to reach maturity through self-dedication and discipline, and to find at the end of the physical existence the world of ineffable light—that is the only way to attain fullness of meaning.

If this is to be our belief, we must also recognize that all peoples must strive for such an objective. And then all else, the luxury of private wealth, the might of nations, will become subordinate; the spirit of man will triumph and liberate itself—his historic task will be completed.

If that is not to be, and yet by some magic wand of progress men find inexhaustible sources of profit, some weapon that in a second can kill millions of enemies, some potion that can keep mortal bodies alive for centuries,—what then, what then?

—1906

The mountain remains unmoved
by its seeming defeat by the mist.

Rabindranath Tagore

BIBLIOGRAPHY

Ajai Singh. Rabindranath Tagore, His Imagery and ideas. Vimal Prakashan, pp. 232, 1984.

Andrew Robinson. The Art of Rabindranath Tagore: A Biographical Study. Macmillan. pp. 157, 1916.

Basanta Koomar Roy. Rabindranath Tagore: The Man and His Poetry. New York Oodd, Mead & Company. pp. 223, 1915.

Benoy Gopal Ray. The Philosophy of Rabindranath Tagore. Hind Kitabs, pp. 155, 1949.

E. J. Thompson, Rabindranath Tagore, His Life and Work: Calcutta: Association Press (Y.M.C.A.). pp. 112, 1921.

Ernest Rhys. Rabindranath Tagore: A Biographical Study. Macmillan, pp. 157, 1916.

Hiren Mukerjee. Himself a True Poem: A Study of Rabindranath Tagore. People's Publishing House, pp. 152, 1961.

K. R. Srinivasa Iyengar. Rabindranath Tagore. Popular Prakashan, pp. 110, 1965.

Kalyan Sen Gupta. The Philosophy of Rabindranath Tagore. Ashgate Publishing, pp. 103, 2005.

Katherine Henn. Rabindranath Tagore: A Bibliography. Scarecrow Press. pp. 631, 1985.

Kedar Nath Mukherjee. Political Philosophy of Rabindranath Tagore. S. Chand and Company, pp. 395, 1982.

Krishna Dutta; Andrew Robinson (editor), Selected Letters of Rabindranath Tagore. Cambridge University Press. pp. 561, 1997.

Krishna Dutta; Andrew Robinson, Rabindranath Tagore: The Myriad-Minded Man. New York: St. Martin's Press, pp. 493, 1996.

Krishna Kripalani, Rabindranath Tagore: A Biography, New York: Grove Press. pp. 417, 1962.

Marjorie Sykes. Rabindranath Tagore. Longmans, Green & Co., pp. 134, 1943.

Mohit Chakrabarti, Rabindranath Tagore: Diverse Dimensions. Atlantic Publishers & Distributors. pp. 191, 1990.

Mohit Chakrabarti. Rabindranath Tagore: A Quest. Gyan Publishing House, pp. 155, 1995.

Mry M. Lago. Rabindranath Tagore. Twayne. pp. 176, 1976.

Niharranjan Ray. An Artist in Life: A Commentary on the Life and Works of Rabindranath Tagore. University of Kerala, pp. 480, 1967.

Patrick Colm Hogan; Lalita Pandit (editor). Rabindranath Tagore: University and Tradition, Fairleigh Dickinson University Press, pp. 297, 2003.

Rajendra Verma, Rabindranath Tagore: Prophet Against Totalitarianism, Asia Publishing House, pp. 84, 1964.

Sasadhar Sinha. Social Thinking of Rabindranath Tagore. Asia Publishing House. pp. 198, 1962.

Sisirkumar Ghose. Rabindranath Tagore. Sahitya Akademi. pp. 131, 1986.

Sujit Mukherjee, Passage to America: The Reception of Rabindranath Tagore in the United States, 1912-1941, Bookland, pp. 239, 1994.

T. R. Sharma. Perspectives on Rabindranath Tagore, Vimal Prakashan, pp. 206, 1986.

Tapati Dasgupta. Social Thought of Rabindranath Tagore: A Historical Analysis. Abhinav Publications, pp. 230, 1993.

Uma Das Gupta. Rabindranath Tagore: A Bibliography. Oxford University Press, pp. 104, 2004.

Vishwanath S. Naravane. An Introduction to Rabindranath Tagore. Macmillan Co. of India, pp. 180, 1977.

INDEX